SHEPHERD'S NOTES

SHEPHERD'S NOTES

When you need a guide through the Scriptures

Deuteronomy

BROADMAN
&HOLMAN
PUBLISHERS

Nashville, Tennessee

0–8054–9027–2
Dewey Decimal Classification: 222.15
Subject Heading: BIBLE. O.T. DEUTERONOMY
Library of Congress Card Catalog Number: 97–37020

Library of Congress Cataloging-in-Publication Data

Deuteronomy / Paul Wright, editor.
      p. cm. — (Shepherd's notes)
    Includes bibliographical references.
    ISBN 0–8054–9027–2
    1. Bible. O.T. Deuteronomy—Study and teaching.   I. Wright, Paul,
1955— .   II. Series
BS1275.5D48   1998
222'.1507—dc21   97–37020
                                                    CIP

1 2 3 4 5 6   03 02 01 00 99 98

CONTENTS

FOREWORD

Dear Reader:

Shepherd's Notes are designed to give you a quick, step-by-step overview of every book of the Bible. They are not meant to be substitutes for the biblical text; rather, they are study guides intended to help you explore the wisdom of Scripture in personal or group study and to apply that wisdom successfully in your own life.

Shepherd's Notes guide you through the main themes of each book of the Bible and illuminate fascinating details through appropriate commentary and reference notes. Historical and cultural background information brings the Bible into sharper focus.

Six different icons, used throughout the series, call your attention to historical-cultural information, Old Testament and New Testament references, word pictures, unit summaries, and personal application for everyday life.

Whether you are a novice or a veteran at Bible study, I believe you will find *Shepherd's Notes* a resource that will take you to a new level in your mining and applying the riches of Scripture.

In Him,

David R. Shepherd
Editor-in-Chief

DESIGNED FOR THE BUSY USER

Shepherd's Notes for Deuteronomy is designed to provide an easy-to use tool for getting a quick handle on this Bible book's important features, and for gaining an understanding of its message. Information available in more difficult-to-use reference works has been incorporated into the *Shepherd's Notes* format. This brings you the benefits of many advanced and expensive works packed into one small volume.

Shepherd's Notes are for laymen, pastors, teachers, small group leaders and participants, as well as the classroom student. Enrich your personal study or quiet time. Shorten your class or small group preparation time as you gain valuable insights into the truths of God's Word that you can pass along to your students or group members.

DESIGNED FOR QUICK ACCESS

Bible students with time constraints will especially appreciate the time-saving features built into the *Shepherd's Notes*. All features are intended to aid a quick and concise encounter with the heart of the message.

Concise Commentary. Deuteronomy is a pivotal book. It is rich with instruction for God's people, designed to equip them for living in the Promised Land. Short sections enable you to grasp quickly the essentials of this book that was so important in the life of Jesus and which gives insight into what God desires for His people today.

Outlined Text. A comprehensive outline covers the entire text of Deuteronomy. This is a valuable feature for following the flow of the book, allowing for a quick, easy way to locate a particular passage.

Shepherd's Notes. These summary statements appear at the close of every key section of the narrative. While functioning in part as a quick summary, they also deliver the essence of the message presented in the sections which they cover.

Icons. Various icons in the margin highlight recurring themes in Deuteronomy, aiding in selective searching or tracing of those themes.

Sidebars and Charts. These specially selected features provide additional background information to your study or preparation. These include definitions as well as cultural, historical, and biblical insights.

Maps. These are placed at appropriate places in the book to aid your understanding and study of a text or passage.

Questions to Guide Your Study. These thought-provoking questions and discussion starters are designed to encourage interaction with the truth and principles of God's Word.

In addition to the above features, study aids have been included at the back of the book for those readers who require or desire more information and resources for working through Deuteronomy.

DESIGNED TO WORK FOR YOU
Personal Study. Using the *Shepherd's Notes* with a passage of Scripture can enlighten your study and take it to a new level. At your fingertips is information that would require searching several volumes to find. In addition, many points of application occur throughout the volume, contributing to personal growth.

Teaching. Outlines frame the text of Deuteronomy, providing a logical presentation of the message. Capsule thoughts designated as "Shepherd's Notes" provide summary statements for presenting the essence of key points and events. Application icons point out personal application of this message, and Historical Context icons indicate where background information is supplied.

Group Study. *Shepherd's Notes* can be an excellent companion volume to use for gaining a quick but accurate understanding of the message of a Bible book. Each group member can benefit by having his or her own copy. The *Note's* format accommodates the study of or the tracing of the major themes in Deuteronomy. Leaders may use its flexible features to prepare for group sessions or use them during group sessions. "Questions to Guide Your Study" can spark discussion of Deuteronomy's key points and truths.

LIST OF MARGIN ICONS USED IN DEUTERONOMY

 Shepherd's Notes. Placed at the end of each section, a capsule statement that provides the reader with the essence of the message of that section.

 Old Testament Reference. Used when the writer refers to Old Testament Scripture passages that are related or have a bearing on the passage's understanding or interpretation.

 New Testament Reference. Used when the writer refers to New Testament passages that are related to or have a bearing on the passage's understanding or interpretation.

 Historical Background. To indicate historical, cultural, geographical, or biographical information that sheds light on the understanding or interpretation of a passage.

 Personal Application. Used when the text provides a personal or universal application of truth.

 Word Picture. Indicates that the meaning of a specific word or phrase is illustrated so as to shed light on it.

Although Deuteronomy is usually thought of as a book of laws, it is really something quite different. Deuteronomy is a book of religious and ethical instruction for ancient Israel. Its teachings were aimed at helping the Israelites—God's people—live wise and godly lives at home, at work, and in their neighborhoods. Persons who aligned themselves with the instructions of Deuteronomy became good family members and fine citizens.

AUTHOR AND DATE OF WRITING

Nowhere does the Book of Deuteronomy explicitly state the name of its author. Nevertheless, there is good reason to believe that Deuteronomy was the product of Moses.

The tradition of Mosaic authorship of the Pentateuch is based primarily on the witness of Deuteronomy itself. Numerous references to Moses speaking and even writing the words of Deuteronomy are found within the book (see 1:1, 5; 5:1; 27:1; 29:2; 31:1, 9, 24, 30; 33:1). Apparently, later Old Testament writers and Jesus Himself accepted the Mosaic authorship of the Pentateuch whenever they spoke of "the law of Moses" (see Josh. 1:7–8; 1 Kings 2:3; 2 Kings 14:6; 2 Chron. 25:4; Ezra 3:2; Luke 24:44).

The issues regarding the authorship of the Pentateuch are complex and should not be lightly brushed aside. However, Christians, as followers of Christ, do well to embrace the same high view of the Scriptures which Jesus held. The books of the Pentateuch, including Deuteronomy, can be understood to make good sense historically and theologically with Moses as the

The title of the fifth book of the Bible, *Deuteronomy*, comes from a Greek word that means "second law." This title is based on an early Greek translation of the phrase, "A copy of this law," found in Deut. 17:18. The name of the book in Hebrew, the language in which it was written, is "These are the words," the book's opening phrase.

The life principles contained in Deuteronomy extend well beyond ancient Israel, however. They also inform Christians—God's people today—how to live lives which are pleasing to God in the midst of the complexities of the twenty-first century.

The title of the book of Deuteronomy in some English translations, "The Fifth Book of Moses Called Deuteronomy," is not part of the inspired text of the Bible. Rather, this title reflects an early Jewish and Christian tradition. According to this tradition, Moses wrote the five books of the Pentateuch (Genesis, Exodus, Leviticus, Numbers, and Deuteronomy) during the time that Israel wandered in the wilderness prior to their conquest of Canaan.

Moses lived in either the fifteenth or thirteenth century B.C. The life of Moses is dated by evidence which first dates the Exodus from Egypt and the conquest of Canaan by Joshua. This evidence, which includes literary, historical, archaeological, and social scientific data, is complex and largely inconclusive.

author and the contemporaries of Moses as his first intended audience.

While it is proper to speak of Moses as the author of the Pentateuch, there is evidence within the Bible that he was guided by the influence of the Holy Spirit to use existing written or oral sources for some of his information (see Num. 21:14). In this way Moses' literary activity was similar to that of Luke (Luke 1:1–4). Other verses in the Pentateuch suggest a minimal amount of editorial "updating" after the death of Moses, such as the account of Moses' death and burial (Deut. 34:1–12). However, the substance of the Pentateuch, and especially the Book of Deuteronomy, must be seen as Mosaic.

Except for Jesus, no character towers above biblical history higher than does Moses. While Moses' biography can be written largely from data provided in Exodus and Numbers, the Book of Deuteronomy provides a special look at his life as God's spokesman. In Deuteronomy, the voice of God and the voice of Moses sound as one. Moses spoke the divine word as teacher (1:5; 4:5; 6:1) and prophet (18:15; 34:10–12) to Israel. Moses was God's chosen servant (3:24; 34:5). He also functioned as an intercessor who felt deeply—one could even say "suffered"—on behalf on his erring people (9:6–10:11). [From Patrick D. Miller, Jr., "'Moses My Servant': The Deuteronomic Portrait of Moses" *Interpretation* 41 (1987): 245–255.]

AUDIENCE

The five books of the Pentateuch, all written by Moses and tied together in structure and theme, were originally intended to be read as a single work by a specific audience. That audience was the generation of Israelites who were poised to enter the Promised Land.

The Israel which Moses faced at the twilight of his career was confronting significant changes. Gone was the difficult life of slavery in polytheistic Egypt. Nearly over was forty years of wandering in the wilderness. Israel had entered into a covenant relationship with the one true God a generation earlier at Mount Sinai. Now they were on the threshold of receiving their own land, Canaan, and setting into motion all of the social, political, economic, and religious structures which were to accompany settled life. This was to be *their* Promised Land, given by God Himself so that His chosen people, Israel, might live full and blessed lives and draw others to Him (Gen. 12:1–3). But Canaan was a strange land to the Israelites, presenting numerous challenges to their physical, social, and spiritual well-being.

PURPOSE

Perhaps the greatest crisis which the people of Israel faced as their time in the wilderness drew to a close was a change in leadership. Moses was about to die and Joshua, rather than Moses, would lead the Israelites into Canaan. The entire Pentateuch, but especially the Book of Deuteronomy; was to be a perpetual witness to the covenant relationship which God had freely entered into with Israel at Mount Sinai (4:13; 31:24–26). For this reason it was imperative that Moses entrust to Joshua in written form the revelation that he had received from God (31:7–29).

Together, these five books of the Pentateuch are often referred to as the Torah. *Torah* is a Hebrew word which is usually translated "law."

God, the divine author of the Pentateuch, guided Moses so that his words would speak with relevance not just to the Israelites of Moses' day but also to audiences of all generations. Later Old Testament writers such as Hosea and Jeremiah were deeply influenced by the Book of Deuteronomy. Jesus quoted it often, including three times when He was tempted by Satan (Matt. 4:4, 7, 10; cp. Deut 8:3; 6:13, 16). Altogether the writers of the New Testament quoted, cited, or alluded to Deuteronomy more than two hundred times. Today pious Jews recite the *Shema* (6:4), the great confession of monotheism, every morning and evening. Christians as well profit greatly by reading and carefully considering the divine instructions contained in Deuteronomy.

3

Much of the Pentateuch contains statutes, ordinances, and commands which were intended to regulate the personal, social, and religious lives of the ancient Israelites (see Exod. 20:1–31:17; Leviticus; Num. 18:1–19:22; Deut. 12:1–25:19). God's covenant at Mount Sinai, in fact, has been called ancient Israel's "constitution."

Not every situation requiring legal guidance which arose in ancient Israel had a specific corresponding statute in the Pentateuch, however. The legal material in the Pentateuch contains greatly detailed information for some situations (e.g., matters relating to worship and social justice) and very little for others (such as marriage and divorce). It appears to be not a complete code of laws but a paradigm to guide the Israelites in their relationship with God and each other. By knowing the laws of the Pentateuch well, ancient Israel could decide other matters as they arose (see 19:4–6). That is, the legal material of Deuteronomy was intended not just to regulate, but also to instruct and to guide. Partly for this reason, the word *Torah* is often better translated "teaching" or "instruction."

The Hebrew word *torah*, which is usually translated "law" in English Bibles, is derived from a word which means "direction," "guidance," or "instruction." A better translation of *torah* is "teaching." In the Bible the word *torah* is used in a number of contexts, from a wise man teaching his son (Prov. 3:1) to God teaching Israel (Isa. 1:10). The English word *law* tends to have negative connotations ("you've got to do it!") while the word *teaching* has positive connotations ("let me show you how, so you'll want to do it!"). The latter is much more consistent with the intended spirit of the Pentateuch (cp. Deut. 30:6; Rom. 15:4).

With this in mind, the purpose of Deuteronomy becomes clear. That purpose is stated in Deut. 1:5: "Moses began to expound this law." That is, Deuteronomy is an *explanation* of the law, not merely a repetition of it as the title *second law* ("Deuteronomy") might otherwise suggest.

Deuteronomy consists primarily of sermons delivered by Moses. These sermons offered ancient Israel a guidebook for living in the land of Canaan. They did this by applying existing principles of behavior which were grounded in God's covenant to new situations which the people of Israel would face once they arrived in Canaan. In many ways, then, Deuteronomy is something like a commentary on already known laws.

Through his sermons, Moses called Israel to again hear God's Torah (instructions) and make a new commitment to Him (6:5). Because of Israel's experiences in the wilderness, Moses knew that the Law could not be kept through external effort. Rather, Israel's commitment to God was to issue from the heart (30:6).

"The Lord your God will circumcise your hearts and the hearts of your decendents, so that you may love him with all your heart and with all your soul, and live" (Deut. 30:6).

STRUCTURE AND CONTENT

The structure and content of Deuteronomy is tied to the overall structure and content of the Pentateuch, the larger work for which it forms a conclusion. Each of the books of the Pentateuch contributes necessary theological elements to the development of its overall theme—the redemption and restoration of God's people:

BOOK	THEMATIC FOCUS
Genesis 1–11	Beginnings
Genesis 12–50	Promise
Exodus	Redemption
Leviticus	Holiness
Numbers	Testing
Deuteronomy	Instruction

The Book of Deuteronomy is composed primarily of four sermons, a song, and an extended blessing delivered by Moses to Israel on the plains of Moab across the Jordan River from Jericho (cp. Num. 35:1; 36:13). These discourses were given a short time before Israel crossed the Jordan to begin their conquest of Canaan. In each discourse, Moses provided important instructions for Israel relevant to their upcoming life in the Promised Land. Specifically, these instructions were aimed at explaining the ramifications of the covenant relationship which God and Israel had entered into at Mount Sinai.

DISCOURSE	TOPIC	REFERENCE
Moses' First Sermon	Remembering the past	1:5–4:40
Moses' Second Sermon	Getting ready for the present	4:44–26:19
Moses' Third Sermon	Consequences of obedience	27:1–28:68
Moses' Fourth Sermon	Looking to the future	29:2–30:20
Moses' Song	Praise	31:30–32:43
Moses' Blessing	Blessings on the twelve tribes	33:1–29

The Hittites were a large and influential people group in the second millennium B.C. whose homeland was on the Anatolian plateau (modern central Turkey). During the time of Moses, the Hittites had formed a large and powerful empire which vied with Egypt for control over the eastern Mediterranean seaboard. Early in the fifteenth century B.C., the Hittites codified their laws. In the early thirteenth century, they fought a major battle with Egypt at Kedesh on the Orontes River (in modern Lebanon) which was concluded with a peace treaty.

Moses' second sermon, by far the longest, forms the core of Deuteronomy. In this sermon, Moses first recited the Ten Commandments (5:6–21) and then explained, in their proper order, what each of the commandments meant for life in the Promised Land.

There is a general consensus that the specific order in which the six discourses of Moses were placed in the Book of Deuteronomy was modeled after a type of ancient covenant treaty called a suzerain (or vassal) treaty. The ancient Hittites drew up suzerain treaties with their conquered vassals in order to stipulate the rights and obligations which applied to each party. These treaties typically contained certain components which are also found in Deuteronomy in the same general order:

- preamble (1:1–5)—furnishes the setting for the treaty;

- historical prologue (1:6–4:49)—reviews the events which led to the formation of the treaty;
- general stipulations (5:1–11:32)—gives the basic principles defining the relationship between the treaty parties;
- specific stipulations (12:1–26:19)—provides specific statutes to guide the relationship between the treaty parties;
- blessings and curses (27:1–28:68)—outlines the consequences for keeping or breaking the terms of the treaty; and
- witnesses to the treaty (30:19, 31:19; 32:1)—testifies to the commitments made by the treaty parties.

Why would Deuteronomy, a book of instructional discourses, be structured according to a vassal treaty? A vassal treaty was drawn up in the ancient Near East when a great power (usually a king) wanted to establish certain conditions of vassalage on a weaker power (usually a king or a people conquered in battle). God had established a covenant relationship with the people of Israel at Mount Sinai (4:13). Moses used a known treaty form to express the nature of that relationship to Israel. God, the absolute sovereign, imposed certain obligations on Israel, His people but at the same time obligated Himself to care for them. Actions signal commitment to a relationship, and obedience to God's laws by Israel served to validate their commitment to the covenant.

LITERARY STYLE

Deuteronomy tells a story, but only chapter 34 can properly be called a narrative. The story told is not so much one of events that *had* happened (although a record of historical events is found in chapters 1–4 and in scattered places throughout chapters 5–11) but of things which *would*

The Book of Deuteronomy is easier reading than the other legal sections of the Pentateuch. This is because the book is written in a broad homiletical style, as preaching or exhortation. In Exodus, Leviticus, and Numbers, God spoke to Moses and gave Israel a set of laws; in Deuteronomy, Moses spoke to Israel *about* the laws which God had already given.

happen, or—depending on Israel's level of obedience to God—*might* happen to Israel. With Moses, the Book of Deuteronomy peered across the Jordan River into the land of Canaan and anticipated the future story of Israel.

Moses' words were passionate. He cited laws, spoke blessings and curses, and composed poetry. Each of these was aimed at motivating Israel to respond favorably to the demands of their covenant relationship with God. Together, Moses' sermons served as his farewell address, spoken with all the conviction and urgency of a man desperately wanting his people to do well.

THEOLOGY

Deuteronomy is a theologically rich book that can be appreciated only by carefully reading (and re-reading!) it, first in the context of the Pentateuch, then with reference to the entire Old Testament, and finally in light of the New Testament. Many foundational biblical truths are proclaimed by Deuteronomy, such as:

- monotheism (6:4);
- the sovereignty of God over people and nature (3:1–3, 18; 11:11–17; 28:1–6, 15–19);
- the love of God for people and our love in response to Him (1:31; 7:7–8; 11:1–12; 30:20);
- the solidarity of God's covenant people (14:27–29; 15:7–11); and
- the importance of heartfelt, ethical behavior in everyday life (6:4–5; 10:16–20; 30:6).

The theological message of Deuteronomy is grounded in the concept of covenant. The covenant which God established with the children of Israel at Mount Sinai bound Him and His people together in close relationship. Israel's divine "chosenness" entailed certain rights and responsibilities (7:6–11; 10:12–15). Israel was made into God's "treasured possession" (7:6; cp. Exod. 19:5–6) and given special instructions to help them live rightly in their Promised Land (5:1–25:19). In return, they were expected to obey God's commands (27:9–10). If they did so, they would be blessed (28:1–14); but if they failed to obey, they would be punished (i.e., "cursed") and driven out of their land (28:15–68). God's blessing to Israel under the terms of the covenant established at Mount Sinai, therefore, was conditional, based on Israel's obedience to the terms of the covenant.

Moses knew that the people of Israel would not be able to keep God's laws through their own effort. For this reason, he spoke of Israel's need to receive a "circumcised heart" (10:16; 30:6), a metaphor for faith in God.

Deuteronomy, the last book of the Pentateuch, has close theological ties to the first book of the Pentateuch, Genesis. In Genesis, God promised Abraham, Isaac, and Jacob that their descendants would become a great nation and inherit the land "from the river of Egypt to the great river, the Euphrates" (Gen. 15:18; cp. Gen. 12:1–3; 13:14–17; 17:6–8, 16; 22:17–18; 26:3–4; 28:13–15; 35:10–12). At the end of the Book of Deuteronomy the nation of Israel stood at the threshold of this, their God-created and God-given Promised Land.

The land belonged to God but was given to Israel as a gift to possess (1:25; 5:16, 31; 12:1). God was to be so identified with His people and their land that He would make His "name" (i.e., character or essence) dwell there (12:11;

A covenant is a compact between two parties mutually binding them to certain agreed upon obligations and benefits. Scripture refers to a number of covenants drawn up between various persons or nations. Some covenants were instituted by God; these include covenants made with Noah (Gen. 9:9–17), Abraham (Gen. 15:17–21; 17:2, 9–14), Moses (Exod. 19:5–6), David (2 Sam. 7:12–16; cp. 23:5), and the New Covenant of Jeremiah (Jer. 31:31–34). Although the form and details of these divine covenants differed, their basic content remained the same: "I shall be your God, you shall be my people, and I will dwell in your midst" (cp. Gen. 17:7; Exod. 6:6–7; 19:4–5).

14:23). Like the garden of Eden, the land was a "good" (1:25; cp. Gen. 1:31) and delightful place in which to live (11:9; 26:15; cp. Gen. 1:29). The land was a place of "rest" (12:9–10) where every seventh day Israel could remember that God "rested" and enjoyed His creation (5:12–15; cp. Exod. 20:8–11; Gen. 2:1–3). This special focus on land in Deuteronomy spoke to the Israelites' need for "belongingness" and security.

THE MEANING OF DEUTERONOMY FOR TODAY

Deuteronomy graphically portrays the character of God, the sinful nature of man, and the possibility of restoration through the grace of God. Because such things do not change, the principles of Deuteronomy help Christians to better understand God, themselves, and the world.

It was almost 3,500 years ago that Moses stood before Israel on the plains of Moab and spoke the words which became known as the Book of Deuteronomy. Although Moses' words were shaped to meet specific needs of his contemporaries, they remain relevant for Christians today. In the fourth century A.D., St. Augustine said, "The law of God was necessary not only for the people of that time but remains necessary now for the right ordering of our lives as well" (*Contra duas epistolas Pelagianos,* 3.10). At the turn of the twenty-first century, the need for Christians to hear again the laws of God remains strong.

Many of the "problems" which Christians face in finding relevance in Deuteronomy center on the legal material which dominates so much of the book. Is there a distinction between Mosaic Law that is universal and timeless (i.e., moral law) and Mosaic Law that is culture- and time-bound (civil and ceremonial law)? Though such a distinction is often made by modern interpreters of the Bible, it is not so clearly stated in Scripture. Even the New Testament church had difficulty determining the extent to which the Mosaic Law must be followed by those living under Jesus' New Covenant (see Acts 15:1–29).

The Ten Commandments (5:6–21) are usually held to apply to all Christians; but one of them, "Observe the sabbath day by keeping it holy" (5:12–15), appears to be a culture-bound ceremonial law. What should a Christian's response to the laws of the Old Testament be?

Christians do well to realize first that the legal material of Deuteronomy, as Torah, is better understood not as law *per se* but as God's instructions for life in the Promised Land (see "Purpose" above). By following these instructions, the ancient Israelites learned what it meant to live lives that were pleasing and acceptable to God.

So it is for the Christian. The Torah continues to demonstrate God's expectations for His people, even though the particular circumstances of life in the Western world today are radically different than they were in the ancient Near East. The Old Testament law is applicable to Christians in the sense that by it we can learn what God expects of us in our relationship with Him and with others. Jesus helped us learn how to use the Mosaic legislation when He accepted, then internalized, the Law in the Sermon on the Mount (Matt. 5–7; cp. Matt. 22:34–40). Most importantly, Jesus kept the Law from His heart, a faith-based attitude that Moses had intended all along (10:16; 30:6).

In this way, even the ceremonial law has relevance for Christians. When Paul urges Christians to "offer your bodies as living sacrifices, holy and pleasing to God" (Rom. 12:1), he is calling for the same kind of relationship that God was seeking to maintain with Israel through sacrifice. While the physical mechanism that expressed that relationship has changed, the basis of the relationship—faith in God—has not.

Deuteronomy also holds meaning for Christians because it speaks of the Messiah. The concluding assessment of Moses' life, "Since then, no prophet has risen in Israel like Moses, whom the

LORD knew face to face," (34:10), anticipates a future prophet who would one day surpass even Moses (18:15–22; cp. Matt. 13:17). That one is Jesus Christ, a prophet greater than Moses (John 1:45; 7:40; Acts 3:22–26; 7:37) because He is God's son (Heb. 1:1–2; 3:1–6).

Moses was a picture (or type) of Jesus. Jesus' work was similar, but far superior, to that of Moses. Moses was God's servant (34:5), but Jesus was God's Son (Heb. 3:1–6). Moses spoke to God "face to face" (34:10), but Jesus knew God even more intimately because He *was* God (Luke 10:22; John 1:18). Moses was a miracle worker (34:11–12), but Jesus' miracles were greater and more numerous (Matt. 11:2–5). Moses earnestly prayed that God would preserve an erring Israel (9:18–20), but Jesus daily intercedes to God on behalf of a sinful world (1 Tim. 2:5; Heb. 4:14–16). Moses was a lawgiver (5:1–25:19) but Jesus mediated a New Covenant (Heb. 8:5–7; 9:15; 12:24; cp. Matt. 5:17–48). Moses delivered Israel from bondage in Egypt (11:2–4) but Jesus delivers all people from the bondage of sin (Luke 4:18; Rom. 5:12–21; 7:24–25; Heb. 7:27).

The opening five verses of Deuteronomy form a preamble to the book similar to the preambles which customarily introduced ancient Near Eastern vassal treaties (see "Introduction, Structure, and Content" above).

MOSES' FIRST SERMON

REMEMBERING THE PAST (DEUT. 1:1–4:43)

Deuteronomy is a forward-looking book. Each of Moses' sermons anticipated the day when Israel would be settled in their Promised Land. His words saw the potential for a great future which lay open, like an unread scroll, before Israel.

Yet Moses began Deuteronomy by speaking about the past. By highlighting certain events from the recent history of ancient Israel—many of which were vividly recalled by Moses' audience—he was able to illustrate graphically just what the covenant relationship that God had established with His people would involve.

The Setting of Deuteronomy (Deut 1:1–5)

Moses spoke to Israel east of the Jordan River on the plains of Moab (1:5; cp. Num. 35:1; 36:13), forty years after the Exodus from Egypt (1:3) and subsequent to Israel's defeat of Sihon and Og, two powerful kings who lived in Transjordan (1:4). Most of the place names listed in verse 1 cannot be identified; they are probably stopping places in the Aravah on the way from Horeb (1:2) to Moab (1:5). The first day of the eleventh month (1:3) occurred in our middle to late January.

- "These are the words Moses spoke to all Israel" (1:1).

- "Moses proclaimed to the Israelites all that the LORD had commanded him concerning them" (1:3).

- "Moses began to expound this law, saying" (1:5).

With these words, Deuteronomy established a clear and deliberate line of authority which passed from God to Moses to Israel. Moses would speak God's words directly to Israel and interpret them in a way wholly consistent with the previous revelation which he had received at Mount Sinai (Exod. 19–24). In this way, the validity of Moses' words was grounded not in himself or even in the covenant-making revelation of Sinai, but in the reality of God.

Aravah in the Bible is the term used to designate the great Rift Valley between what are now the countries of Israel and Jordan.

In the Bible the term usually refers to the Jordan River valley north of the Dead Sea (see Deut. 3:17; 2 Kings 25:4–5), but in modern times Arabah designates the extension of the Rift Valley south from the Dead Sea to the Gulf of Aqaba. Horeb (lit. "dryness") is the name for Mount Sinai which is preferred by Deuteronomy. It occurs nine out of the ten times that Mount Sinai is mentioned in the book. Moab is the region immediately east of the Dead Sea, and the term *Transjordan* refers to all the land east of the Jordan River, an area approximately corresponding to the modern country of Jordan.

Jewish tradition of the early centuries A.D. extended this line of divine authority in an unbroken chain from Moses to the present. This is stated in an ancient Jewish book of instruction called "Sayings of the Fathers:" "Moses received the Torah on Sinai, and handed it down to Joshua; Joshua to the elders; the elders to the prophets; and the prophets handed it down to the men of the Great Synagogue." Judaism holds that, in the never-ending search to make God's words relevant, modern rabbis speak with as much authority as did Moses.

■ *At the very end of Israel's period of wilder-*
■ *ness wanderings, Moses undertook to*
■ *explain to Israel what God's covenant*
■ *required of them once they entered the Prom-*
■ *ised Land. Moses' explanation comprises the*
■ *Book of Deuteronomy.*

THE JOURNEY FROM MOUNT SINAI TO THE PLAINS OF MOAB (DEUT. 1:6–3:29)

Moses' first sermon reviewed events from the past forty years of Israel's history. He spoke first of instances of disobedience and judgment, but then reminded Israel of times when they had been obedient and God had blessed. This portion of Deuteronomy forms the historical prologue section of the vassal treaty format which provides the basic structure of the book (see "Introduction, Structure, and Content").

The Wilderness Wanderings (1:6–46)

Moses' sermon opened with a warning. Disobedience had led an entire generation of Israelites, as it would Moses, to die outside the Promised Land.

The Departure from Sinai (1:6–8)

The history of Israel recorded in Deuteronomy began not with the Exodus from Egypt but with the departure from Mount Sinai, here called Horeb (1:6). That is, it began with the covenant which God had established with Moses and the people of Israel already in place. While the Israelites were still at Horeb, God told Israel that it was time for them to take hold of the land which

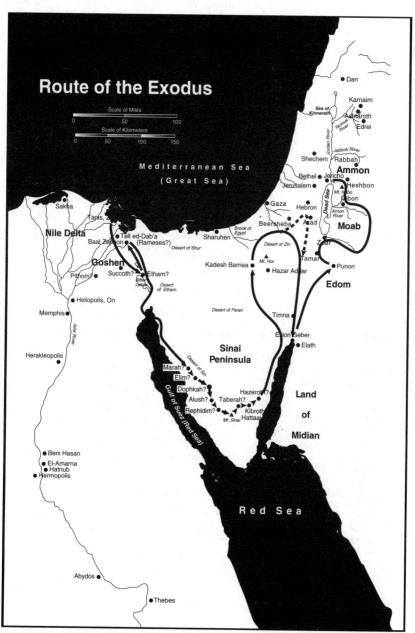

Adapted from *Holman Bible Handbook*, (Nashville, Tenn.: Broadman & Holman Publishers, 1992), p. 169

He had promised to give to Abraham, Isaac, and Jacob (1:8; cp. Gen. 15:18).

An immediate conquest of the land of Canaan *could* have happened. Israel had their chance at entering the land of their inheritance, but unbelief, and then disobedience, caused God to postpone the fulfillment of His promise. Moses' audience, standing on the plains of Moab and getting ready to try to enter the Land of Promise again, knew this all too well.

- *From Horeb God told Israel to journey on.*
- *That journey, like all of life's pilgrimages*
- *undertaken at the prompting of God, held*
- *great promise. God offered all things good,*
- *but Israel would soon choose trouble.*

The Appointment of Leaders for Israel (1:9–18)

Because Moses was not able to bear personally all of the numerous "problems, burdens and disputes" (1:12) which accompanied so great a multitude, he appointed a judiciary to operate under him (1:13; cp. Exod. 18:13–27; Num. 11:10–17; Deut. 16:18–20). The men of the judiciary, chosen for their wisdom, understanding, and experience, were commanded to judge righteously and without partiality, "for [such] judgment belongs to God" (1:13, 16–17).

By reminding Israel of the distribution of authority among their elders at the beginning of his first sermon, Moses sought to make three things clear from the outset:

1. The need to appoint additional leaders was a good thing that had arisen only

Later biblical prophets often appealed to the ideal figure of a righteous judge when they decried the social ills of their day. In words reminiscent of the spirit of Deuteronomy, Isaiah cried out, "Learn to do right! Seek justice! Encourage the oppressed! Defend the cause of the fatherless! Plead the cause of the widow!" (Isa. 1:17). Too often, however, justice was corrupted in the very courts which were ordained for it to be upheld (Prov. 22:22–23; Isa. 59:4; Amos 2:7; 5:15).

because God had fulfilled His promise to make Israel a mighty nation (1:11; cp. Gen. 12:2; 22:17).

2. As a covenant community Israel had to share certain responsibilities. The cooperation of everybody for the common good was necessary to benefit all.

3. In spite of the appointment of effective leaders, the people of Israel still rebelled against God (cp. 1:19–46). The problem lay not with the system of leadership but with each individual heart.

- *Through Moses, God appointed capable*
- *leaders for His people. With effective leader-*
- *ship and a devoted populace, Israel's future*
- *looked bright.*

THE SPIES AND ISRAEL'S UNBELIEF (1:19–46)

Eleven days out of Horeb, Israel arrived at Kadesh-barnea, a large oasis in the northeastern Sinai peninsula (1:19; cp. 1:2). From there Moses sent spies into Canaan, the land of the Amorites, to scout out the land for Israel's anticipated occupation (1:20–25; cp. Num. 13:1–33). The spies brought back a good report, but the people did not believe the land could be taken and so rebelled against both Moses and God (1:26–33). As a result, God condemned Israel to wander about "through all that vast and dreadful desert" (1:19) until everyone who was of the age of accountability—with the exception of Joshua and Caleb, who had believed—had died (1:34–40). Israel refused to accept their punishment and tried to invade

"Amorite"

Throughout the early chapters of Deuteronomy, the inhabitants of Canaan are called Amorites rather than Canaanites. *Amorite* comes from a word found in ancient Near Eastern documents meaning "the West," referring to the region west of Mesopotamia. In the Bible the term *Amorite* often denotes all the inhabitants of Canaan (as in Deut. 1–4) but other times refers just to those who lived in the hill country (see Num. 13:29).

Canaan anyway, but were defeated in battle (1:41–46; cp. Num. 14:39–45).

Moses' account of Israel's rebellion at Kadesh-barnea in Deuteronomy 1 added an emphasis not found in the story as it was first reported in Numbers 13–14. In Deuteronomy, Moses was careful to emphasize the goodness of God in providing for Israel (1:21, 25, 30–33), comparing God's care to that of a father for his own son (1:31). It was the sons and daughters of the unbelieving Israelites, "children who do not yet know good from bad" (1:39), who would next have a chance to enter their Promised Land. These children were now wilderness-toughened adults, standing ready and eager to succeed where their parents had failed.

Moses intentionally chose the phrase "children who do not yet know good from bad" (1:39) to described those who would eventually enter the Promised Land. This phrase did not indicate that the children were below the age of accountability, but it contained an allusion to Moses' description of the tree of the knowledge of good and evil in the garden of Eden (Gen. 2:17; 3:5). This tree was placed off-limits to Adam and Eve in order to teach them that God alone has both the ability and the right to know what is good and what is not good for people. By continually refusing to submit themselves to God's right-to-know, the adult Israelites at Kadesh-barnea, like Adam and Eve, were banished from their special land.

■ *Moses brought the forty-year old story of*
■ *Israel's unbelief up to date by emphasizing*
■ *the role that the children—now responsible*
■ *adults—had in God's plan to inherit*
■ *the land.*

THE CONQUEST AND SETTLEMENT OF TRANSJORDAN (2:1–3:39)

After wandering in the wilderness for almost forty years (2:14), God offered Israel a new chance to enter the land of Canaan. This time, the promise made to Abraham four centuries earlier (cp. Gen. 12:1–3; 15:13) was set to be fulfilled.

The Approach Through Seir and Moab (2:1–23)

Moses quickly passed over the generation-long period of wilderness wanderings (2:1; cp. Numbers 16–20) to emphasize Israel's advance through southern Transjordan to the plains of Moab.

God told Moses to lead Israel through Seir (or Edom; 2:4–8) and Moab (2:9–15).

Israel then approached the border of Ammon (2:16–23) but was told not to contend with them either, for they too had descended from Lot and as such had received their land from God (2:19; cp. Gen. 19:36–38).

It was important for later Israelites to know why the lands of Seir (Edom), Moab, and Ammon were never conquered or apportioned as an inheritance for the twelve tribes of Israel. These lands remained Israel's eastern enemies throughout the time of the Old Testament (see Judg. 3:12–14; 7:22–8:17; 11:4–33; 1 Sam. 14:47; 2 Sam. 8:2–12; 2 Kings 3:4–5; 2 Chron. 20:1–37).

Moses made a special chronological note in connection with the crossing of the Israelites into Moab. The journey from Kadesh-barnea to the rugged Zered River valley, the southern boundary of Moab, took thirty-eight years (2:14). During this time, the "entire generation of fighting men" who had not believed the spies' report died. By making this note, Moses confirmed that God's spoken judgments are sure (cp. Num. 14:20–23), and hinted that when Canaan was conquered, it would be by the strength of God, not military might.

Seir and Moab were two lands southeast and east of the Dead Sea which lay in the path of the Israelites' final approach to Canaan. Israel was not to fight with the inhabitants of either land (2:5, 9) because God had given Seir to the descendants of Esau (2:5; cp. Gen. 32:3; 36:6–9) and Moab to the descendants of Lot (2:9; cp. Gen. 19:36–38).

■ *By not allowing Israel to conquer the territo-*
■ *ries of Seir, Moab, or Ammon, God was*
■ *faithful to the promises which He had made*

- *centuries before during the time of the patri-*
- *archs. Although these countries lay outside*
- *of His chosen line, God's purposes for history*
- *included their welfare.*

Victories over Sihon, King of Heshbon, and Og, King of Bashan (2:24–3:11)

The Amorite king Sihon had established a kingdom based at Heshbon, a city on a plateau between Moab and Ammon just east of Israel's intended destination on the plains of Moab (Num. 21:26). God told Moses to begin the conquest of Israel's Promised Land by taking the kingdom of Sihon (2:24–25). Sihon provoked war when he, with a hardened heart, refused Israel passage through his land (2:26–30). Israel defeated Sihon by the power of God and captured all of his land, from the Arnon River that empties into the Dead Sea to the Jabbok River that flows into the Jordan, fifty miles to the north (2:31–37).

Moses then defeated Og, the king of Bashan, who controlled the high and fertile region lying east of the Sea of Galilee and stretching from the Jabbok River north to Mount Hermon (3:1–10).

Bashan was a kingdom of strong cities (3:5) and its king a man of renown, whose huge iron bed became a "museum piece" even in antiquity (3:11). Yet he, like Sihon, was defeated by the power of God (3:2–3).

The description of the defeat of Sihon and Og is graphic and, for modern sensibilities, rather shocking (2:33–35; 3:3–7). According to Moses, "We took all his towns and completely destroyed them—men, women and children. We left no survivors" (2:34). All this was done at the command of God (2:31; 3:2; cp. Gen. 15:16). Why would God command

Much of this region today is part of the Golan Heights.

The defeat of Sihon and Og entered deeply into the consciousness of ancient Israel. Songs praising the mighty acts of God made particular mention of Israel's victory over these two kings (Ps. 135:10–12; 136:17–22). When Ezra blessed the Jews after they had rebuilt the walls of Jerusalem following their return from the Babylonian Exile, he specifically mentioned the defeat of Sihon and Og as evidence that the land belonged to Israel (Neh. 9:22).

such an act when a simple defeat of the trained armies of Sihon and Og would have given Moses the land?

These battles, and several others which Israel would fight once in the land of Canaan (see Josh. 6:15–21; 1 Sam. 15:1–33; cp. Deut. 7:1–5), are referred to by the term *holy war* . A holy war was a battle commanded by God to completely destroy a people already living in the Promised Land who belonged to another god. Such people stood to undermine God's purposes for Israel. A holy war was primarily a religious act and had to follow certain guidelines. The practice of holy war was limited to a short period of Israel's history and in no way serves as a paradigm for Christian behavior today, except to underline the exclusive holiness demanded by God and to recognize that ultimately He is the victor over all sin.

"Completely Destroy"

The Hebrew term translated "completely destroy" means literally "to ban" or "to devote" to God people or objects who were thoroughly hostile to Him. The concept of the ban is related to the idea of holiness, or total separation from things that are evil. By placing a city and its inhabitants "under the ban," they became God's exclusive property to dispose of as He saw fit.

■ *The defeat of Sihon and Og cleared the way*
■ *for Israel to begin settling in the Promised*
■ *Land. Untimately, their victory could be*
■ *explained only by the sovereignty of God*
■ *over His creation.*

The Tribal Inheritance in Transjordan (3:12–22)

After defeating the kingdoms of Sihon and Og, God instructed Moses to apportion their land to two and one-half of the Israelite tribes (3:12–17; cp. Num. 32:1–42). The tribes of Reuben and Gad received the land which had been taken from Sihon. This land was particularly well suited to cattle grazing, which formed the economic base of these tribes (Num. 32:1–5). Jair

Without faith in Jesus, persons are already condemned (John 3:18) and remain under the wrath of God (John 3:36). By participating in holy war, Israel acted as God's agent of divine wrath (Gen. 15:16). Moses was clear that Israel, too, was not exempt from divine judgment (Deut. 27–28); if they failed to believe, they would also be removed from their land (4:26).

Eventually, said Moses, God would give "rest" to all Israel (3:20; cp. 12:10). This "rest," the goal of Israel's journey to the Promised Land, would be reminiscent of the "rest" which God experienced after creating that—and all—lands (Gen. 2:1–3), and which characterized life in the Garden of Eden.

and Machir, two clans from the tribe of Manasseh (hence the designation "the half-tribe of Manasseh" in 3:13; cp. 1 Chron. 2:21–23), received the land which had belonged to Og.

After apportioning their land, Moses made sure that Reuben, Gad, and the half-tribe of Manasseh knew their responsibility to aid the other Israelite tribes in conquering the land west of the Jordan River (3:18–20; cp. Josh. 22:1–9). Moses reassured Joshua that God would fight for him once Israel crossed into Canaan (3:21–22).

■ *With the conquest of the lands in Transjor-*
■ *dan and their apportionment to various Isra-*
■ *elite tribes, the promise of land which God*
■ *had made to Abraham four centuries earlier*
■ *(Gen. 12:2; 15:16–21) began to be fulfilled.*

Moses Denied Entrance to the Promised Land (3:23–29)

Moses' charge to Joshua was not to fear but to be strong and of good courage when leading Israel against the Canaanites (3:22, 28; 31:7–8). God's charge to Joshua after the death of Moses used the same words (31:23; Josh. 1:5–9).

Moses, who had lived long (cp. 31:2; 34:7) and witnessed many mighty acts of God, was awestruck at the great things that yet lay in store for Israel: "O Sovereign LORD, you have [only] begun to show to your servant your greatness and your strong hand!" (3:24). Moses begged God to allow him to at least see the Promised Land, but God refused (3:25–26). Moses could only view the land from afar. God would charge Joshua to lead Israel into Canaan (3:27–28; cp. 34:1–4).

Moses did not specify the reason why God would not allow him to enter Canaan other than to say that "because of you the LORD was angry with me" (3:26; cp. 1:37; 4:21). Later in the book, Moses reported that God told him that Moses had broken faith in not upholding His holiness before Israel (32:51). This Moses had done by co-opting God's power when he faced a rebellious Israel in the wilderness of Zin (Num. 20:2–13; 27:12–14). In the end, Moses, too, forfeited the Land of Promise.

- *Moses, not to be an exception because of his*
- *high position of leadership, faced the conse-*
- *quences of his actions, just as all people do.*
- *Yet God was gracious and allowed him at*
- *least to see the land for which he longed.*

MOSES' CALL TO OBEDIENCE (DEUT. 4:1–40)

Moses issued a passionate call to obey God following his recitation of key events which led Israel to the point of entering the Promised Land. This call was based on past actions, on the choices which faced Israel in the future, and on the character of God.

A Call to Obey Based on the Past (4:1–24)

Moses called on Israel to heed and obey God so they might live and enter the Land of Promise (4:1). Moses first illustrated the need to obey by offering warnings from the past. He carefully interspersed his call for obedience with stated (or implied) examples of Israel's former unbelief: the sexual idolatry at Baal-peor (4:3; cp. 23:17–18; Num. 25:1–4; Ps. 106:28–31); the golden calf incident at Mount Sinai (4:15–17; cp. Exod. 32:1–35), and the rebellion in the wilderness of Zin which had tripped up even him (4:21; cp. Num. 20:2–13).

The connection between wisdom (4:6) and fearing God (4:10) was made often by the biblical writers. The clearest statement, "The fear of the Lord is the beginning of wisdom," is found several places in the Old Testament (Job 28:28; Ps. 111:10; Prov. 1:7; 9:10). To be wise was to conform oneself to the will of God.

Moses gave a second reason to keep God's statutes: doing so would "show your wisdom and understanding to the nations" (4:6). Israel's wisdom, their skill in living, came from divine revelation, not human reasoning. By remembering the awesome appearance of God at Mount Sinai, Israel would learn how to fear Him (4:10–11, 24). By obeying the instructions (Torah) which God revealed at Mount Sinai, Israel would learn how to live (4:12–14). The nations round about would see and respond favorably to Israel (4:7–8), for God had long ago promised that they would be blessed by the descendants of Abraham (Gen. 12:3).

■ *Moses called Israel to live in obedience to*
■ *God so they could live in the Promised Land*
■ *and draw other nations to Him. This was the*
■ *essence of the promise which God had made*
■ *to Abraham (Gen. 12:1–3).*

A Call to Obey Based on the Future (4:25–31)

Having surveyed the past, Moses now looked to the future. The past generation had not believed God. Would future generations, the "children and grandchildren" (4:25) of Moses' audience, do any better? Moses warned that, should Israel continue to choose not to believe or obey, they would be driven out of the Promised Land and would live among the idolatrous nations (4:26–28).

Moses established the principle of responsible behavior in the face of conditional promises. God's people are expected to be faithful to Him, but in His sovereignty God is not obligated to bless those who disobey. This was understood by the apostle Paul, who wrote, "As a prisoner for the Lord, then, I urge you to live a life worthy of the calling you have received" (Eph. 4:1; cp. Col. 1:10), and, in the spirit of Deuteronomy: "Find out what pleases the Lord" (Eph. 5:10).

Moses' "If you sin" (4:25) could well have been "When you sin." In Genesis, Moses had written of how Adam and Eve (Gen 3:24) and Cain (Gen 4:16) were exiled from their special lands; he now anticipated the future exile of Israel to

Assyria (2 Kings 17:1–20) and Judah to Babylon (2 Chron. 36:11–21).

But God is gracious. If Israel would sincerely return to Him, He would certainly forgive and restore them (4:29–31). The pattern of rebellion—retribution—repentance—restoration became common during the period recorded in the Book of Judges. The clearest call, however, was made by the writer of Chronicles: "If my people, who are called by my name, will humble themselves and pray and seek my face and turn from their wicked ways, then will I hear from heaven and will forgive their sin and heal their land" (2 Chron. 7:14).

- Moses had great expectations for Israel's
- future, but he knew that God's blessings were
- conditional, based on Israel's obedience and
- belief. Nevertheless, God was gracious and
- would not forget His covenant.

A Call to Obey Based on the Uniqueness of God (4:32–40)

Moses ended his first sermon by calling on Israel to obey simply because of who God is. Through a series of rhetorical questions, Moses led Israel to realize that God is totally and absolutely unique (4:32–34). No other god speaks audibly, without man-made form (4:33, 36; cp. Exod. 19:18; 20:1). No other god redeemed a miserable people from slavery and forged them into a great and feared nation (4:34, 37–38). No other god cares enough for people to discipline and love them (4:36–37). No other god, in fact, even exists (4:35, 39). For these reasons alone, Israel ought to respond with obedience (4:40).

"Do it! . . . Because I said so, that's why!" This approach isn't very effective for parents to use with their children, and it isn't used by God with His children, either. Rather, God's approach is relational: "I love you, I made you, I've done great things for you, and I care for you every day, so I also know what's best for you."

- *The call to obedience is grounded ultimately*
- *in God's sovereign power and His love and*
- *concern for His people. The past and the*
- *future may be untouchable, but the possibil-*
- *ity for a relationship with God is very much*
- *in the present.*

The Cities of Refuge in Transjordan (Deut. 4:41–43)

The cities of refuge were places where a person who committed manslaughter could flee and wait until his case could be fairly judged (Num. 35:12–15; Deut. 19:4–21; Josh. 20:3–6). This important provision, which was grounded in the sanctity of the individual, was aimed at curtailing blood revenge. The actual use of these cities as places of refuge is not documented in Scripture.

Moses listed the three cities of refuge in Transjordan as an appendix to his first sermon. This was an appropriate place for the list because his first sermon focused on the conquest and settlement of Transjordan by Israel (cp. 2:1–3:22). Joshua would designate three more cities of refuge in the land of Canaan according to the instructions of Moses (Josh. 20:1–9; cp. Deut. 19:1–3), thereby bringing the total to six (cp. Num. 35:10–15).

- *By providing cities of refuge, God showed*
- *Himself to be both gracious and just. By*
- *instilling these same qualities in His people,*
- *God sought to establish a righteous society.*

QUESTIONS TO GUIDE YOUR STUDY

1. Why was it important for Moses to bring up the past? What did the past teach Israel about God? About themselves? About their children?

2. Were the covenant blessings which God promised to Moses automatic? On what were they based?

3. What did Moses say in his first sermon about himself? About leadership in general? About following the leadership of others? Of God?

MOSES' SECOND SERMON - - - - -

GETTING READY FOR THE PRESENT (DEUT. 4:44–26:19)

Moses' second sermon is the longest in the Book of Deuteronomy. In it he sought to prepare Israel for life in the Promised Land, soon to be a very present reality. This Moses did by explaining how the Ten Commandments which God had given at Mount Sinai were to be relevant for Israel's new, landed life in Canaan. Moses first restated the Ten Commandments (5:1–21), then provided general principles (6:1–11:32) and specific stipulations (12:1–25:16) which issued from them.

The contents of this sermon correspond to the main section of the ancient vassal treaty form on which the Book of Deuteronomy was based (see "Introduction, Structure, and Content"). This section of the vassal treaties carefully stipulated the principles and guidelines which defined the relationship between the treaty parties—God and Israel in this case. The superior party, God, expected the lesser party, Israel, to obey. In return, Israel would be cared for by God.

THE HEART OF THE COVENANT (DEUT. 4:44–5:33)

The Ten Commandments form the heart of God's covenant. In compressed form they contain everything that God demands of His people. In addition, they are a window to the character of God. By incorporating the Ten Commandments into the Sermon on the Mount (Matt. 5:21–48), Jesus upheld their validity for Christians.

The Covenant Setting (4:44–49)

Moses introduced the covenant by summarizing its content, its origin, and the locale in which it was delivered to Israel.

Moses described the content of the covenant as "laws," literally "Torah" or "instruction" (4:44; see "Introduction, Purpose"). Specifically, this instruction contained statutes, decrees, and ordinances (4:45), things commanded by God. As divine sovereign, God holds the right to command obedience. His people, on the other hand, learn how to live by listening to Him and doing (obeying) what He commands.

This instruction came from Moses (4:45), who had received it directly from God (5:2–5). It was delivered to Israel on the plains of Moab, here called "the valley near Beth Peor" (4:46; cp. 34:1), across the Jordan River from Jericho, after Israel had conquered the lands in Transjordan belonging to Sihon and Og.

The Ten Commandments were given to a redeemed community, persons already standing in a right relationship with God (5:6). They were never intended to be a means of salvation or a means of finding acceptance in the eyes of God. Rather, the commandments were to be Israel's expression of faith in God.

■ *By explaining the Ten Commandments to*
■ *Israel, Moses prepared them for life in the*
■ *Promised Land.*

The Ten Commandments (5:1–21)

Moses spoke to the point: the covenant which God made at Mount Sinai was for the present, "[for] us, all of us who are alive here today" (5:3). Its immediacy is evident.

The form of the Ten Commandments as spoken by Moses in Deuteronomy is virtually identical to that recorded in Exodus 20, except that the reason given for keeping the Sabbath in Deuteronomy was to remember Israel's redemption from Egypt rather than the seven days of creation (5:15; cp. Exod. 20:11).

The commandments may be divided into two sections. The first four speak of Israel's relationship to God. Their overall theme is the worth and worship of God alone. The last six treat interpersonal relationships. They establish the principle that all people are of inestimable value and as such have rights which must be protected.

Throughout the remainder of his sermon, Moses explained what each of the Ten Commandments meant to Israel. Because the first two commandments formed the basis for the rest, they received extensive treatment in chapters 6–12 of Deuteronomy. Matters relating to the rest of the commandments followed in order, in chapters 13–25.

"The Ten Commandments" is an English translation of the Hebrew phrase *the Ten Words* (4:13; 10:4; cp. Exod. 34:28). The term *decalogue* comes from a Greek phrase meaning the same thing. The title *Ten Words* reveals the commandments to be much more intimate and compelling than a mere divine order. As words of God, they issue from the very essence of His being. Creation also originated with the words of God (Gen. 1:3). Throughout biblical history, God continued to speak until He finally spoke through His own Son, the Word (John 1:1–3; Heb. 1:1–2). The connection between the creation, Jesus, and the Ten Commandments—God's words of instruction for life—cannot be broken (Matt. 5:17).

- *The Ten Commandments, the very words of*
- *God, provide all of the necessary principles*
- *by which God's people may live lives pleas-*
- *ing to Him. As Moses made the command-*
- *ments relevant for ancient Israel, so Jesus did*
- *for the New Testament community.*

Moses, the Covenant Mediator (5:22–33)

Upon hearing the voice of God boom from Sinai, a mountain enveloped in fire and thick darkness, the Israelites were overcome with fear (5:22–26; cp. Exod. 20:18–20). They begged

The description of Mount Sinai as surrounded with both fire and thick darkness is somewhat paradoxical. Many understand this as a theophany (an appearance of God) in the form of a volcanic eruption or violent thunderstorm. While this is possible, the combination of fire (destroying light) and thick darkness has important theological overtones. Fire indicates the all-consuming power and self-revelation of God (Ps. 97:3–4). While darkness is usually associated in the Bible with trouble, punishment and death (see Ps. 107:10; Matt. 8:12), thick darkness suggests the inexplicable mystery of God (1 Kings 8:12; Ps. 97:2).

Moses to approach the mountain in their place lest they be consumed by the fire of God, then agreed in desperation to hear and obey everything God commanded them to do (5:25–27). God's response was passionate: "Oh, that their hearts would be inclined to fear me and keep all my commands always!" (5:29). The type of fear (terror) that the Israelites experienced was not the type of fear (reverence) which God expected of them.

Moses then received from God the specific decrees, statutes, and ordinances by which he was to teach Israel how to live after they had arrived in the Promised Land (5:31). These laws form the bulk of the book of Deuteronomy.

Israel recognized that a great gulf lay between themselves and God. There was a dire need for an intermediary to bridge that gap. That intermediary was Moses, who willingly mediated God's covenant to Israel (5:28–31). In doing so, he foreshadowed Jesus, who freely mediated God's new covenant to all who believe (1 Tim. 2:5; Heb. 9:15; 12:24).

- *Moses received God's laws and delivered*
- *them to Israel. Israel's proper response was*
- *to walk with God, and their reward would be*
- *a long and blessed life in the Promised Land.*

PRINCIPLES OF THE COVENANT (DEUT. 6:1–11:32)

Chapters 6–11 of Deuteronomy provide, in broad homiletic style, the principles for life on which the covenant stipulations found in chapters 12–25 are based. These principles derive directly from the first two commandments:

"You shall have no other gods before me" (5:7) and "You shall not make for yourself an idol. . . .You shall not bow down to them or worship them" (5:8–9). As was his habit in Deuteronomy, Moses illustrated these principles by selected events taken from Israel's past.

Without a proper view of God, everything else comes out wrong. The first two commandments establish who God is and why He demands exclusive devotion from His people.

A First Principle: God's People Must Love Him and Keep His Commandments (6:1–25)

Moses began his exhortation on the basic principles of the law with the *Shema*: "Hear, O Israel: The LORD our God, the LORD is one" (6:4). The *Shema*, which is recited twice daily by pious Jews, comprises the essence of ancient Israelite and Jewish religion. This confession proclaimed the unity and uniqueness of the Lord God. In using the plural pronoun "our," it also affirmed that the Lord is God of a community of believers.

Because the Lord God is totally unique, He demands total and exclusive allegiance by His people. This Moses expressed with the command to "love the LORD your God with all your heart and with all your soul and with all your strength" (6:5). On more than one occasion, Jesus quoted this command when asked what was the heart of the Law, and those to whom He spoke obviously agreed (Matt. 22:34–40; Mark 12:28–34; Luke 10:25–28).

The commands to hear (6:4) and to do (6:5) were followed by a command to teach (6:7–9). Without faithfully entrusting God's revelation to each new generation, His people would cease to exist (see 2 Tim. 2:2). The repetition "when you

Shema

Shema is the Hebrew command "hear," the first word of Deut. 6:4. The command to "hear" or "give ear" typically introduced formal addresses of great import (cp. 32:1; Judg. 5:3; Isa. 1:2). Hearing and doing were inseparable actions for Moses (5:1, 31; 6:5–6). To hear and not obey was not to hear at all, and not to obey was to fail to receive God's blessing. Jesus agreed (Luke 11:28).

Strength

The Hebrew word which is translated by the English nouns *strength* (NIV) or *might* (NKJV) in Deut. 6:5 is actually an adverb meaning "much" or "very." Moses used an adverb rather than a third noun after "heart" and "soul" because any other noun was inadequate to express the "very muchness" with which God called His people to love Him.

sit . . . when you walk . . . when you lie down . . . when you rise" recognized that all of life is lived as a clear testimony to one's children (Ps. 1:1–2).

God was giving Israel a land in which other people were already living; as sovereign Creator, this was His right (32:8–9). One of the benefits of receiving the land of Canaan was that it was ready for human habitation: cities, houses, water cisterns, and vineyards were already in place (6:10–11). Twice in these verses Moses used the word *good* to describe this specially prepared land, an allusion to the goodness of creation (Gen. 1:4, 31) and the specially prepared garden in which Adam and Eve had also walked with God.

A literal understanding of verses 8–9 has led many people to place copies of Deut. 6:4–9 on their forehead, hand, or doorposts. Moses' intent, however, was that Israel know the law of God so well that it would become "impressed on one's mind" and be "always at hand."

The drawback of Canaan, Moses knew, was that the Canaanites' false gods would entrap Israel. To believe in the uniqueness of the Lord God meant that Israel must not in any way acknowledge that the gods of other peoples were true gods, for to do so would mean the end of God's covenant people (6:12–15).

Moses emphasized the need to love God and keep His commandments by citing two historic events. The first was the rebellion at Massah in which Israel, fresh out of Egypt, failed to believe that God could (or would!) provide for their needs in the wilderness (6:16–19; cp. Exod. 17:1–7). The second was the Exodus from Egypt (6:21–23; cp. Exod. 5:1–15:21). It was only because of God's mighty acts of deliverance that Israel now stood at the edge of the Promised Land and enjoyed a covenant relationship with God. Israel's proper response was to understand (6:20) and obey (6:24–25).

- *Because the Lord is the only God, His people*
- *must respond with complete and exclusive*
- *devotion to Him. The claims of God shaped*
- *Jesus' ministry, and they should do no less for*
- *His followers today.*

For ancient Israel, the "no other gods before me" (5:7) were the false gods of Canaan. While graven images or idols (5:8) seldom tempt Christians today, a host of other, more subtle things take their place. A person's god is anything to which they devote all of their time, energy, and obedience. Whatever is most important in life is a god—and for many Christians, that thing too often is not God.

A Second Principle: God's People Must Not Associate with Other Gods (7:1–26)

The dangers which the false gods of Canaan held for ancient Israel were very real. Moses foresaw that the everyday contact which Israel would have with the Canaanites would draw God's people away from Him (7:4, 25). For this reason, Israel was commanded not to intermarry with the Canaanites (7:3) and to destroy the objects of pagan religious worship which they found in Canaan (7:5, 25).

Moses also told Israel to wipe out the Canaanites: "You must destroy them totally. Make no treaty with them, and show them no mercy" (7:2; cp. 7:16, 24). Israel was to treat the Canaanites in the same way they had dealt with Sihon and Og (cp. 2:33–35; 3:3–7). Moses gave the reason for this holy war against Canaan in verse 6: "For you are a people holy to the LORD your God." The exclusive holiness of God demanded, at least at this point in their history, that Israel be totally separated from pagan religious systems.

The Bible offers several explanations for holy war: to reduce the threat of apostasy (7:4, 25); to punish the Canaanites for their advanced state of sinfulness (9:4–6; cp. Gen. 15:13); and to provide a safe and secure home for the people whom God loved (7:6–8).

For many in today's age of tolerance, it is difficult to understand God's command to destroy the Canaanites. After all, isn't religious fanaticism something to be avoided? Haven't enough wars been fought over differing views of religious truth? A sensitive reader feels the pain of the Canaanites—these were real people with hopes and dreams for their own future—yet also recognizes the sovereignty of God in the matter (cp. Isa. 55:8–9).

To reduce a deity to wood and stone (5:8) was to limit its character ("my god looks and acts just like this") and power ("I can pick up my god and do with him as I please"). For this reason, anything that we do which limits or circumscribes God—that holds Him to be less than what He is—is a violation of the second commandment. Ultimately it is the all-encompassing sovereignty of God, and that alone, that explains holy war.

Although the call for holy war is difficult for many Christians to understand, it must be accepted as appropriate, given the time and circumstances of ancient Israel's founding. Neither God nor the biblical writers apologized for the reality of holy war, and no attempt was made in the Bible by a later editor to clean up the text to fit a more "politically correct" mood.

Ancient Israel was a unique people in a unique time and place in history. Their exclusivity was a channel for God's blessing (7:12–15). But with the establishment of the New Covenant under Jesus, God's blessing has been opened to all who believe in Him (Gal. 3:28–29). Neither holy war nor a rigid separation from all things of the world are real options for Christians today; Jesus, after all, ate with publicans and sinners (Mark 2:15–17). God only demands that His people be holy (1 Pet. 1:15) and not conform to the ways of the world (Rom. 12:2).

■ *Moses called Israel to separate themselves*
■ *totally from pagan Canaanite religious prac-*
■ *tices. By doing so, a dangerous temptation to*
■ *reduce the one true God to Canaanite forms*
■ *of worship was eliminated.*

A Third Principle: God Provides What His People Need (8:1–20)

Again and again Moses returned to this theme: for Israel there was a connection between obeying God's commandments and their receiving His blessing in the Promised Land (8:1). This time in order to make the connection, Moses emphasized the goodness of God's provision for Israel during the wilderness wanderings and the goodness of the land which He was providing for them.

God showed His goodness to Israel in the wilderness by disciplining them "as a man disciplines his son" (8:5). That is, by correcting and guiding Israel, God showed that He cared for them enough to prepare them to be a mature people (8:16). He did this by leading Israel through a desert land, a land without adequate food or water, where they could not possibly survive through their own efforts alone.

God let Israel suffer hunger, thirst, and want, then supplied their physical needs (8:2–4, 15–16; cp. Exod. 16:1–17:7). This He did so Israel would not become spoiled by the ease which comes from self-sufficiency, but instead recognize that "man does not live on bread alone but on every word that comes from the mouth of the LORD" (8:3).

It was important that Israel learn that material possessions and wealth come from God, *before* they entered their Promised Land. The reason was that the land which Israel was entering was a land in which "you will lack nothing" (8:9), a land with ample water and mineral resources to sustain life (8:7–9). As a result, said Moses, Israel would eat and be full, and bless the Lord God for the good land He had given them (8:10).

Or so they should. In fact, Moses warned that once they were in the Promised Land, Israel might be tempted to forget the lessons of the wilderness and credit themselves for their life of ease (8:11–17). Who needs to trust in God, after all, when things are going well? Moses repeated the warning He had already made numerous times in Deuteronomy: if Israel

"Affluence is not inherently evil, but it is inherently dangerous. . . Israel's greatest treasure is not gold and silver, but the memory of a time of poverty that demonstrated God's love and humankind's dependence."

Thomas W. Mann, *The Book of the Torah*, (Atlanta: John Knox Press, 1988), 151.

The metaphor of God as a devouring fire emphasized His all-consuming power and absolute intolerance for sin. The biblical writers often used fire to speak of the wrath of God in judgment against the wicked (see Ps. 21:9; 89:46; 97:3; Isa. 30:30; Jer. 4:4; Lam. 2:4; Ezek. 21:31; Zeph. 3:8; Heb. 12:29). In particular, the eschatalogical (end times) Day of the Lord will be accompanied by a fire which issues from God to destroy all wickedness (Dan. 7:9–11; 2 Thess. 1:7–8; 2 Pet. 3:7, 11; Rev. 20:10, 14–15).

would forget the source of their material blessings, they, like the Canaanites, would perish from their land (8:19–20).

■ *Through the wilderness wanderings, God*
■ *brought Israel to a place where they would*
■ *have to trust in Him for survival. Once Israel*
■ *recognized their daily need for God, they*
■ *were able to receive greater blessings of pro-*
■ *vision from Him.*

A Fourth Principle: God Is Faithful in Spite of His People's Unworthiness (9:1–10:11)

Another theme which Moses repeated often in his Deuteronomy sermons was the inherent unworthiness of Israel to receive God's blessings. Israel was smaller and weaker than the nations of Canaan (9:1–2; cp. 7:7, 17). From a strictly human standpoint, the spies had been right in their assessment of Israel's chances of defeating the Canaanites (cp. 1:26–28): they were nil. But because Israel participated in God's covenant, they had only to believe and obey, and God would do the rest.

Israel was small and weak, but God was faithful. Moses had been careful to remind Israel again and again that every aspect of their existence—from the deliverance from Egypt to receiving daily food in the wilderness—was a direct result of God's intervention on their behalf. Because of this, they could be certain that God was capable of going before Israel "like a devouring fire" (9:3; cp. 4:24) to prepare their way in Canaan.

But the primary reason that Israel was unworthy to receive God's blessings was not their size; it was their stubbornness (9:4, 6). Although Moses had already pointed out Israel's failure to believe God in various circumstances (see 1:26–32; 4:21; 6:16–19), he now took up the task with vigor. Moses summed up the entire wilderness experience in verse 7: "Remember this: . . . From the day you left Egypt until you arrived here, you have been rebellious against the LORD."

Moses then gave several examples of Israel's rebelliousness. Chief among these was the uprising at Horeb (Mount Sinai). Before Moses had even finished receiving the terms of God's covenant, Israel had broken their most important element by making and worshiping a molten calf (9:6–21; cp. 5:8–10). Moses responded by smashing the tablets of the covenant into pieces (9:17), for once the covenant had been violated by one of its parties it was technically no longer in force. God had every right to destroy Israel and begin again with a new people (9:13–14), but Moses intervened on Israel's behalf (9:18–20). God remained faithful to the covenant in spite of Israel's unworthiness.

Moses reminded Israel of other instances of rebellion by simply mentioning place names: Taberah (9:22; cp. Num. 11:1–3), Massah (9:22; cp. Exod. 17:1–7), Kibroth hattaavah (9:22; cp. Num. 11:4–34) and Kadesh Barnea (9:23–24; cp. Num. 13:17–14:45). Each of these showed that the incident at Sinai was no fluke, but that Israel had a natural propensity to rebel. Christian theologians call this "original sin."

Moses then repeated to Israel that he had intervened before God on their behalf (9:25–29), and that God had reestablished the broken

The writer of Hebrews compared Mount Sinai, the terrifying mountain where God gave laws which could not be kept, with Mount Zion and the heavenly Jerusalem, the city of God (Heb. 12:18–22). Those who want to participate in Jesus' covenant must remember the warning of Sinai and believe in Him (Heb. 12:25) in order to receive "a kingdom that cannot be shaken" (Heb. 12:28).

covenant by delivering to him new tablets which contained the law (10:1–5). Because of His love for Israel and His faithfulness to the promises which He made to Abraham (cp. 7:6–8; 9:29), God was unwilling to destroy His people (10:10).

■ *God remained faithful to Israel in spite of*
■ *their obvious unworthiness. Because God*
■ *showed His grace in the wilderness, Israel*
■ *knew that He would also be gracious to them*
■ *in the Promised Land. God's faithfulness,*
■ *said Moses, should prompt Israel to be faith-*
■ *ful in return.*

THE FIRST PRINCIPLE RESTATED: LOVE GOD AND KEEP HIS COMMANDMENTS (10:12–11:32)

Moses ended his exhortation on the general principles which issue from the first two commandments by restating the first point which he had made: Israel must love God and keep His commandments (cp. 6:1–25). Moses summarized the essence of the covenant from Israel's side by asking the question, "What does the LORD your God ask of you?" (10:12). His answer was a series of verbs indicating Israel's commitment to God: fear Him, walk in all His ways, love Him, serve Him and keep His commandments (10:12–13). This Israel must do from the heart (10:12, 16), for it was from the heart that God first loved them (10:15).

If Israel would love God with a circumcised heart (10:16) and "hold fast" (12:20) to Him, the result would be a transformed society. Israel would care for the helpless members of society

"Hold Fast"

Moses' command to "hold fast" or "cleave" to God (10:20) used the same verb by which he described the relationship which God intended for a husband and wife: "For this reason a man will leave his father and mother and be united to his wife, and they will become one flesh" (Gen 2:24). The writer of the book of Ruth used the same verb: "Ruth clung to [Naomi]" (Ruth 1:14). Intimate human relationships help us to understand what God desires for the relationship which He established with us.

in the same way that God does (10:17–19), a sure indication that justice and righteousness prevailed in the land.

Moses then prompted Israel to love God by comparing what would happen in the Promised Land with what had happened in the wilderness. In the wilderness, the waters of the Red Sea had "overwhelmed" Pharaoh's army so that they all died (11:4; Exod. 14:26–31). The Promised Land, however, would be a land "[over]flowing with milk and honey" (11:9), rich with provision so that God's people could live. In the wilderness, the earth had opened up and swallowed Dathan and Abiram so that they died (11:6; cp. Num. 16:31–35). The Promised Land, however, would be a land that "drinks (swallows) rain from heaven" (11:11), thereby possessing a God-given fertility which allowed His people to live (11:13–17). Moses warned Israel that their own eyes had seen the trials in the wilderness (11:7), then comforted Israel by reminding them that God's own eyes would be on their new land throughout the year (11:12).

In Egypt, a flat land with no rain, fertility depends on irrigation technology. In antiquity and in some places yet today, water was pumped into canals from the Nile River and thence into fields by foot-propelled paddle-wheel devices (11:10). Israel, a land of hills and valleys, has scant ground water resources. Its rainfall is adequate most years, but often unpredictable.

Theologically, we can say that Egypt was a place where people could live by the strength of their own self-sufficiency, but Israel was—and still is—a land in which its people must depend on the heaven-sent provision of God.

Moses ended his appeal to love God and keep His commandments in the same way that he began, by commanding the Israelites to place the words of the covenant on their hands, foreheads, and doorposts, and to teach them to their

The covenant renewal ceremony was to take place on mounts Gerazim and Ebal and in the valley lying between them (11:29). This region, home to the powerful city-state of Shechem, had figured prominently in the stories of the patriarchs (Gen. 12:6; 33:18; 34:1–31; 35:4; 37:12–14) but was yet unvisited by Israel in Moses' day. For this reason, Moses provided a "roadmap" locating the site (11:30).

children (11:18-20; cp. 6:5–8). In this way, they would be well prepared to inherit the land which had been promised to Abraham (11:24–25; cp. Gen 15:18).

As a closing note, Moses set before Israel "a blessing and a curse" (11:26–28) and spoke of the covenant renewal ceremony which Israel should undertake once they had entered the land of Canaan (11:29–30; cp. Josh. 8:30–35). This note summarized the content of Moses' third sermon, an enumeration of the blessings and the curses which would befall Israel based on their behavior in the Promised Land (27:1–29:1). It also presupposed that the conquest of Canaan would take place just as God had said.

- *By repeating the principle to love God and*
- *keep His commandments, Moses returned to*
- *the heart of the law. Israel's future—whether*
- *one of blessing or of curse—depended on*
- *their adherence to the covenant which God*
- *had graciously established with them at*
- *Mount Sinai.*

QUESTIONS TO GUIDE YOUR STUDY

1. How is the command to love God completely and exclusively the foundation for the whole law?

2. Why did God command Israel to destroy the Canaanite population of the Promised Land?

3. How did Israel's experience in the wilderness teach them that God would provide for their needs once they entered the Promised Land?

SPECIFIC MATTERS RELATING TO THE COVENANT (DEUT. 12:1–25:16)

Having established several basic principles which defined the covenant relationship between God and His people Israel, Moses continued by providing some specific statutes and ordinances which issued from these principles. These were based on each of the Ten Commandments (5:6–21) and arranged generally according to the order of the commandments. The first four commandments concern people's relationship to God, and the last six deal with interpersonal relationships. However, as Deuteronomy 12–25 shows, our relationship with God also has interpersonal, ethical ramifications, and our relationships with each other have important God-ward implications.

This portion of Moses' second sermon contains many laws similar to those already found in the books of Exodus and Leviticus. But Moses was not simply restating legal information which Israel already knew. Rather, he shaped his re-presentation of the law to fit the living conditions which Israel would face in the Promised Land. In his sermon Moses sought to make the law relevant to a new generation of Israel.

Matters Relating to the First and Second Commandments (12:1–31)

"You shall have no other gods before me."

"You shall not make for yourself a graven image."

The statutes and ordinances which Moses established based on the first two commandments all relate to worship.

Moses began and ended this section with a command to avoid the religious practices of the

"The Lord does not give me rules, but He makes His standard very clear. If my relationship to him is that of love, I will do what He says without hesitation. If I hesitate, it is because I love someone I have placed in competition with him, namely, myself. Jesus Christ will not force me to obey him, but I must. And as soon as I obey him, I fulfill my spiritual destiny."

Oswald Chambers, *My Utmost for His Highest*, (Oswald Chambers Publications Association, Ltd., 1992), November 2.

Canaanite religion was a nature-based fertility religion. For this reason, Canaanite sites of worship were out of doors ("on the high mountains and on the hills and under every spreading tree"—12:2) rather than in temples. Archaeologists have found various items of religious paraphernalia associated with Canaanite worship, including altars, incense stands, standing stones, a bronze calf, statues of household fertility goddesses, and molds to cast statues of deities.

Canaanites. Israel was to destroy all Canaanite centers of worship (12:1–3) and not even inquire about their gods lest, by their interest, they "be ensnared to follow them" (12:29–31).

The bulk of Deuteronomy 12 focuses on the centralization of Israel's worship in the Jerusalem temple, here called "the place the LORD your God will choose" (12:5, 11, 14, 18, 21, 26; cp. 1 Kings 8:16–21, 48; 2 Chron. 6:5–6). In order to ensure their separation from Canaanite religious practices and influence, Moses instructed the Israelites to worship in only one place.

Moses commanded that various offerings and sacrifices which had already been described in detail in the Book of Leviticus be brought to this centralized place of worship (12:6, 11, 17, 26–27). When done properly, worship in Jerusalem would be a joyful time of fellowship with God and each other (12:7, 12, 18).

Each of the Ten Commandments, including those which focus directly on God, has an ethical dimension. In the case of the first two commandments, Moses used the occasion of worship to instruct Israel to provide for the physical needs of the Levites (Israel's priests and religious workers) because they were not given their own landed inheritance (12:19).

The "place which the Lord your God will choose" ended up being Jerusalem, but not until the time of David and Solomon, several centuries after Moses' death. Throughout their history the Israelites tended to maintain Canaanite sites of worship, sometimes under the guise of worshiping the Lord God but oftentimes not.

■ *Israel was to avoid everything that had to do*
■ *with Canaanite religion. This included wor-*
■ *shiping in places where Canaanites wor-*
■ *shiped. Israelite religion was to be centered*
■ *on the temple in Jerusalem.*

Matters Relating to the Third Commandment (12:32–14:21)

"You shall not take the name of the LORD your God in vain." (Exod. 20:7; Deut. 5:11, KJV).

In its most narrow sense, the third commandment prohibits swearing an oath (i.e., making a promise) in the Lord's name and then breaking it. In its more broad sense, it forbids any false or unworthy speech or communication about God, or anything that lessens or misrepresents God's name (i.e., His character). It also forbids false speech of any kind.

13:1–18. Moses first spoke of three instances of calumny, the act of uttering false charges with the intent of damaging another person's character. The instances involved a prophet (13:1–5), a family member (13:6–11), and "wicked men" (13:12–18), all of whom might entice Israel to worship other gods. The reputation which was in danger of being defamed, therefore, was God's. In each case the enticing speech would be especially seductive: a prophet is supposed to speak God's words; a family member should be able to be trusted; and base fellows start and fuel delicious rumors. Moses commanded that such persons be put to death (13:5, 9–10, 15–16).

The matter of the false prophet was particularly sensitive for Moses, because he himself was the greatest prophet that Old Testament Israel ever had (cp. 34:10–12). Moses recognized that God would periodically test Israel by sending false prophets (see 1 Kings 22:23), for then Israel would truly have a chance to show that they loved God with all their heart and soul (13:3; cp. 6:5).

14:1–21. Having prohibited one form of apostasy (enticement through false speech to follow

The Hebrew word *vain* used in the third commandment means "emptiness" or "nothingness." When the psalmist declared that idols were "vain," he meant there was absolutely nothing to them. The phrase "in vain" means uselessly, wastefully, falsely, for no reason or to no good purpose.

Not to take the name of the Lord in vain includes not using God's name as a swear word, but much more than that. Everything that we communicate to people about God must be true. Our words should be as trustworthy as His are. If we give our word, we must always keep it. God's people ought to be a people of integrity, in which everything they do is trustworthy and true (Phil. 4:8–9).

The Sabbath was a gift to Israel from God (Mark 2:27) during which people could enjoy rest and peace, and think especially of God. According to Exodus 20:11, the Sabbath was given to remind people of how God rested in the perfection of creation (Gen 2:1–3). It also looks forward to God's people entering His final rest in heaven (Heb 4:9–10). According to Deut. 5:15, the Sabbath was given to remind Israel of their redemption from Egypt; here it also looks forward to the ultimate redemption from sin.

other gods), Moses extended the application of the third commandment to Israel by forbidding other forms of apostasy as well. These included pagan rites of mourning the dead (14:1; cp. Lev. 19:28) and the eating of foods which had been declared in Leviticus to be ritually unclean (14:3–21; cp. Lev. 11:1–47; 17:15). In other societies, only the priests were subject to regulations such as these, but Israel was to be a holy *people* (14:2) where the behavior of each person was to be as blameless as the conduct of its priests.

■ *Israel's speech and actions were to be truth-*
■ *ful at all times, but especially in all things*
■ *which related to God. For Israel to represent*
■ *themselves as God's people and then act in*
■ *ways that harmed the reputation of God*
■ *before others was taken with the utmost*
■ *seriousness.*

Matters Relating to the Fourth Commandment (14:22–16:17)

"Observe the sabbath day to keep it holy."

The fourth commandment regulates formal times of worship. Israel was told to observe the Sabbath, the seventh day of the week, by not working but rather devoting the entire day to God (5:13–14). In addition to the Sabbath, Mosaic legislation in Exodus, Leviticus, and Numbers had added other festivals or special times throughout the year (or cycle of years) during which Israel would have opportunity to focus on God in public worship and celebration (Exod. 23:10–17; Lev. 23:1–44; 25:1–17). Many of these festivals centered on the agricultural calendar of ancient Israel and for that reason could best be observed only in the Promised Land. It was to be expected, then, that Moses would give further instructions regarding Israel's religious festivals just prior to the conquest of Canaan.

14:22–27. Moses first spoke of the law of the tithe (cp. Lev. 27:30–33; Num. 18:21–32). The tithe, one-tenth of a person's yearly produce, was to be set aside to support the Levites. The payment of this tithe included a family celebration in Jerusalem with the Levites, "in the presence of the LORD your God" (14:26).

14:28–29. Moses stipulated an additional tithe to be paid every three years to help support the needy people of the land. Obedience to the fourth commandment thus included an ethical dimension.

15:1–18. Ethical concerns also lay behind Moses explanation of the year of release (sabbatical year) in Deuteronomy (cp. Exod. 23:10–11; Lev. 25:1–7). In an attempt to provide for the poor in Israel (cp. 15:4, 11), Moses stipulated that those who could do so should give freely and ungrudgingly whatever was sufficient for their need. If this were done, additional laws would be unnecessary (cp. 15:5).

However, Moses also provided that those who owed indebtedness, whether monetary (15:2–3) or through indentured servitude (15:12–14; cp. Lev. 25:39), were to be "released" (15:1) every seven years. This release was evidently a cancellation of debts, although it is possible that the release was intended to postpone the terms of indebtedness for one year. In either case, the year of release was a "sabbath" comparable to the weekly day of rest

The Old Testament does not clearly indicate that either the year of release (sabbath year) or the Year of Jubilee (Lev. 25:8–17) was ever kept in ancient Israel. If fact, the writer of 2 Chronicles stated that while Judah was in exile in Babylon "the land enjoyed its sabbath rests; all the time of its desolation it rested" (2 Chron. 36:21). This suggests that the land had a lot of "catching up" to do. The Jews again promised to keep the year of release in the days of Nehemiah (Neh. 10:31), and the first-century historian Josephus reported that they did so periodically during intertestamental times.

The act of eating a sheep or goat as a means of dedicating it to God may seem selfish in today's economy, but it was not at all so in ancient Israel. Meat was almost never eaten in antiquity, especially by the common man, because sheep and goats were used for meeting people's ongoing needs (milk and wool). To kill a sheep or goat just to eat it was to consume one's capital assets foolishly. God demanded that everyone who had sheep or goats give some of them to Him as an offering, then graciously allowed the owner to have the animals back in a feast of great joy.

(Lev. 25:3–4). The justification for both sabbaths was the same: "Remember that you were slaves in Egypt and that the LORD your God redeemed you" (15:15; cp. 5:15).

15:19–23. Moses commanded Israel to dedicate the firstborn animals from their flocks and herds to God by eating them in a family celebration in Jerusalem. The intended context for this meal was probably the Passover (cp. 16:6). The Israelites were to "do no work" with these firstborn animals (not milk or shear them), a clear indication that they, like the Sabbath (Deut. 5:14), were to be holy.

16:1–17. Moses also gave specific instructions governing Israel's three great pilgrimage festivals, Passover (16:1–8), the Feast of Weeks (16:9–12), and the Feast of Tabernacles (16:13–15). Each of these festivals was to be celebrated in Jerusalem by the entire family, and to be accompanied by offerings, sacrifices, and great rejoicing (16:16–17). They were times to thank God for the goodness of the land and His great acts of redemption.

- ■ *God provided regular times of worship for*
- ■ *Israel so His people could celebrate His good-*
- ■ *ness. Once they entered the Promised Land,*
- ■ *most of these celebrations were centered at*
- ■ *the temple in Jerusalem.*

Matters Relating to the Fifth Commandment (16:18–18:22)

"Honor your father and your mother."

The fifth commandment requires that God's people honor their parents. Because Moses was

Festival

Name of festival	Passover (Pesach)	Feast of Weeks/ Pentecost (Shavuot)	Feast of Tabernacles /Booths (Sukkot)
Associated agricultural festival	Feast of Unleavened Bread	Feast of Harvest or Firstfruits	Feast of Ingathering
References in the Pentateuch	Exod. 12:1–28; 23:15; 34:18–20; Lev. 23:5–8; Num. 28:16–25; Deut. 16:1–8	Exod. 23:16; 34:22; Lev. 23:15–21; Num. 28:26–31; Deut. 16:9–12	Exod. 23:16; 34:22; Lev. 23:33–36, 39–43; Deut. 16:13–15
Time of year celebrated	mid-March to mid-April	late May to early June	late September to early October
Historical significance	To remember God's deliverance of Israel out of Egypt	To remember God's deliverance of Israel out of Egypt; in time it also came to commemorate the giving of the law on Mount Sinai	To remember that Israel lived in booths (huts) during the wilderness wanderings
Agricultural significance	Barley harvest celebration	Wheat harvest celebration	General harvest celebration (grains; vine and tree fruits)
New Testament significance	Jesus' last supper was a Passover meal (Luke 22:15); He was also the Passover lamb who brought redemption to the world (1 Cor. 5:7)	Founding of church at Pentecost (Acts 2:1); Christ and believers called "firstfruits" (1 Cor. 15:20, 23; James 1:18)	Attended by Jesus, who used the festival's customary prayers for rain to announce that He was the source of living water (John 7:2, 37–39)

speaking to adults, the honor which is to be shown is not limited to the command, "Children obey your parents," although this is certainly included (cp. Eph. 6:1). Rather, adults must continue to show loyalty and respect to their parents throughout their lives. In its broader aspect, this commandment speaks of care for the elderly and of proper respect for all rightful authority, whether civil or religious.

The fifth commandment is the first one with a promise: "That it may go well with you and that your may enjoy long life on earth" (cp. Eph. 6:2–3). Moses did not mean that there was an automatic connection between honoring one's parents and individual prosperity and long life. He was rather speaking of Israel as a corporate body: If God's people functioned together properly (as evidenced by respect given and received among its members), society would thrive. If not, society would fall apart from within.

The specific statutes which Moses provided in connection with the fifth commandment concerned civil and religious authority structures: the judicial system (16:18–17:13), the king (17:14–20), the priesthood (18:1–8), and prophets (18:9–22). Each of these institutions rose to prominence in Israelite society once Israel became settled in the land of Canaan, and in particular with the establishment of the monarchy under David and Solomon.

The Judicial System (16:18–17:13)

Moses commanded that judges and officers be appointed in every town (cp. 1:9–15), and that these men "judge the people fairly" (16:18–20; cp. 1:16–17). A high court of Levitical priests was established to decide cases which were too difficult for the local judges (17:8–13; cp. Exod.

18:22). As an example of a case requiring judgment, Moses offered an instance of apostasy which might take place "among you in one of the towns" (17:2–7). In such cases, the judges were instructed to inquire diligently into the wrongdoing (17:4) and, if it be a capital offense, hear corroborating testimony from at least two witnesses (17:6), one of whom must also serve as executioner (17:7).

- *Israel's judges were to be fair and impartial*
- *in judgment. Because they were located in*
- *every town, the judges could be sensitive to*
- *individual needs.*

It can be inferred from the words of the biblical prophets that the perversion of justice was a very real problem in ancient Israel. Judges habitually took bribes and showed partiality in judgment, the very things which Moses cautioned against. Amos, more than any other prophet, decried the social injustices which were rampant during the Israelite monarchy. Many of these centered on a corrupt judiciary (Amos 5:10–15, 24).

Kingship (17:14–20)

Moses recognized that, once Israel had entered Canaan, they would want a king to be "like all the nations around us" (17:14; cp. 1 Sam. 8:4–5). The institution of kingship had been anticipated as early as the days of the patriarchs (Gen. 17:16; 35:11; 49:10). Moses provided three statutes to curb abuses of royal power (cp. 17:20):

Later biblical writers judged Israel's kings according to the statutes of Deuteronomy which governed kingship. Solomon's great wealth in horses, gold, and silver (1 Kings 4:26; 9:11, 19; 10:26–29) and many wives (1 Kings 11:3) turned his heart away from God (1 Kings 11:9). In contrast, the good king Josiah read and kept "the book of the law," probably Deuteronomy, a copy of which was found in the restoration of the temple which took place during his reign (2 Kings 22:8–11).

1. The king was to be a fellow Israelite who would, it was supposed, keep the best interests of his people in mind (17:15).

2. The king was not to seek great personal wealth (horses, silver or gold), or take many wives (17:16–17).

3. The king was to copy, read, and keep the laws of Deuteronomy (17:18–19). By doing so, the king would recognize that he was subordinate to God.

First Samuel 2:12–17 provides an example of how the priestly support system changed and developed in ancient Israel (note verse 13: "It was the practice of the priests. . ."). Eli's two sons, Hophni and Phinehas, used their power as priests to extort sacrificial meat for their own use, thereby enriching themselves at the expense of the public.

■ *Israel's kings were not to seek personal*
■ *aggrandizement but to submit themselves to*
■ *the higher authority of God.*

The Priesthood (18:1–8)

In the wilderness, the tribe of Levi had been set aside by God to be priests for Israel (Exod. 32:26–29). They were to serve as intermediaries before God; hence their inheritance in Israel was God Himself rather than land (18:1–2; cp. 10:9). Eventually Joshua would appoint forty-eight cities, four in each of the twelve tribal allotments, as Levitical cities (Josh. 21:1–45; cp. Num. 35:1–8). In this way, the Levites would have a place to call home, and at the same time be evenly distributed among the tribes to serve Israel more effectively.

Because the priests did not engage in extensive agricultural pursuits (cp. Num. 35:2–4), they were dependent on the contributions of others for their support (12:19; 14:27). Moses stipulated that these contributions should be in the form of foodstuffs from the best of Israel's produce (18:3–5; cp. Lev. 7:28–36).

■ *The priesthood served the ongoing religious*
■ *needs of Israel. In exchange for giving them-*
■ *selves to God, they were to receive support*
■ *from the general populace of Israel.*

Prophets (18:9–22)

Regarding prophetic activity, Moses cautioned that "the nations you will dispossess listen to those who practice sorcery or divination"

(18:14). Such activities, specified in verses 10–11, represented an attempt to control the world of the divine. They also focused on death rather than life. For these reasons, Moses called them "detestable practices" to God (18:12) and commanded that they must be avoided by His people (18:9, 13–14; cp. 12:31; Lev. 19:26, 31).

In his instructions relating to the third commandment, Moses had raised the issue of a prophet who would entice Israel to follow false gods (13:1–5). Now he spoke of a true prophet whom God would raise up one day for Israel. That prophet would come from his own people and be like Moses (18:15). He would speak God's words (18:17) so Israel might obey.

The combination of Moses' words in Deut. 18:15–19 and the statement at the end of Deuteronomy that no prophet like Moses had yet arisen (34:10–12) led the Jews to anticipate that the great prophet like Moses would come at the end of time. Upon observing the work and ministry of Jesus in Jerusalem, some of the Jews in the crowd gasped, "Surely this man is the Prophet!" (John 7:40). Deuteronomy 18:18 was taken to refer to Jesus the Messiah by Peter in Acts 3:22–23.

The Hebrew word *prophet* means "spokesman." The prophet was God's spokesman. As a presidential press secretary is commissioned to say exactly what the president would say, so a prophet spoke the very words of God.

Because some prophets would speak God's words while others would not, Moses gave a test by which Israel could determine a true prophet. The test was straightforward: if the predictive word came to pass, the prophet was true; if not, the prophet was false and should die (18:20–22). This test presupposed that the words of prediction referred to the relatively near future, something within the normal life-span of the prophet. Indeed, false prophets normally tried to influence the Israelite king or

The practice of predicting the future through divination was a highly developed and respected art in the ancient Near East. Written documents from Mesopotamia and Canaan speak of various methods of prediction, such as by entering ecstatic trances or by interpreting the design of oil drops on water, the pattern of rising smoke or flying birds, the arrangement of the entrails of animals, or the movement of planets and stars. Such practices were condemned by the biblical writers (Isa. 8:19; 47:9; Jer. 27:9; Mal. 3:5; Rev. 21:8).

people regarding events or conditions which were imminent, and so almost always spoke of the immediate future (see 1 Kings 22:5–28).

■ *Israel's prophets were to look to God for*
■ *guidance rather than depend on methods of*
■ *their own making. As a result, they were*
■ *God's spokesmen.*

Matters Relating to the Sixth Commandment (19:1–22:8)

"You shall not murder."

The commandment not to kill does not forbid all types of killing but only wrongful or unwarranted killing, or killing not sanctioned by the law. Specifically, it forbids murder and manslaughter. Moses used the framework of the sixth commandment also to instruct Israel on related matters such as accidental death, lawful killing (capital punishment), and war.

Intentional and Unintentional Homicide (19:1–21)

19:1–13. The first guideline which Moses established regarding homicide was to call for three additional cities of refuge in Israel (19:1–3, 7–9; cp. Num. 35:9–15). Three cities of refuge had already been designated for use by the tribes who had received their inheritance in Transjordan (4:41–43). Joshua chose the additional cities when the conquest of Canaan had been completed: Kedesh in northern Galilee, Shechem in the central hill country, and Hebron in the southern hill country (Josh. 20:1–9).

A person who committed manslaughter could flee to one of these cities and wait for his case to be fairly adjudicated. In this way, Moses sought to curtail blood revenge (19:4–6). These cities were not, however, intended to harbor persons guilty of premeditated murder. If such a person sought sanctuary in a city of refuge, they were to be extradited and put to death (19:11–13).

The Hebrew word for "kill" found in the sixth commandment is used in the Bible to refer to the killing of individuals, never killing in war or the killing of animals. For this reason, it is better translated "murder" or "manslaughter."

19:14. One of the most common causes of dispute among individuals (and nations!) in the ancient Near East was the encroachment on another's property rights. In order to prevent such disputes, which often led to open conflict and murder (cp. the incident regarding Naboth's vineyard in 1 Kings 21:1–16; and Job 24:1–2), Moses legislated against "removing" (i.e., moving or ignoring) set boundary markers.

19:15–21. In Deut. 17:6 Moses established the need for at least two witnesses in adjudicating a criminal offense. Now in connection with murder, the most serious of crimes against people, he elaborated on this principle. A false witness was to be exposed and made subject to the same punishment as the guilty party for whom he lied.

- *The Law of Moses was unbending in cases of*
- *intentional homicide but merciful if death*
- *was unintentional.*

Warfare (20:1–20)

Moses next provided statutes which regulated the conduct of warfare. These statutes were intended to prepare Israel for its wars of conquest in Canaan as well as other battles that Israel might fight outside its own land. While God deemed the total destruction of Canaan to be necessary, Deuteronomy 20 called for practices of warfare which were more humane than was the norm in the ancient Near East.

20:1. The statutes of warfare which Moses established presuppose that God would be fighting for Israel. If Israel was faithful to God, they need not fear larger, stronger enemies (cp. Josh. 5:13–15; 2 Kings 6:15–19).

20:2–9. Before battle Israel's army was to be blessed and encouraged by a priest (cp. 2 Chron. 20:20–21). Certain men were to be exempt from fighting: anyone who had built a new house and not yet dedicated it, anyone who had planted a new vineyard and not yet enjoyed its fruit, anyone who had just gotten married (cp. 24:5) and anyone who was afraid. Gideon allowed this last exemption as he prepared to fight the Midianites (Judg. 7:2–3).

20:10–18. The rules for warfare for Israel differed, depending on the location of the city to be besieged. When the city was far away, that is, outside the Promised Land, Israel was first to ask for terms of peace. If the besieged city refused, only then could Israel destroy it. Cities within the land of Canaan were to be completely destroyed from the start. This was to be done according to the practice of holy war for which Moses had called in Deut. 7:1–5. The end result was that wars were not to be fought for personal wealth or national aggrandizement, but to eliminate pagan practices which would lead Israel into sin.

20:19–20. The note to spare the fruit trees in the area surrounding a besieged city was necessary to combat the practice of decimating the countryside in order to make siege equipment. It was probably because of conduct such as this that Israel's kings gained a reputation for being merciful to their enemies (cp. 1 Kings 20:31).

■ *Because war was a real part of Israel's*
■ *national identity, it had to be regulated by*
■ *law. When conducted properly, warfare in*
■ *ancient Israel was more humane than war-*
■ *fare conducted by their neighbors.*

Other Cases Related to the Sixth Commandment (21:1–22:8)

The final section of Deuteronomy which was devoted to Moses's explanation of the sixth commandment contains a variety of laws. Some are clearly related to killing; others are more akin to the spirit of the commandment, and they concern situations involving anger, hate, and negligence.

21:1–9. The problem of unrequited justice arose if the identity of a killer could not be determined. In such cases, Moses provided a means by which those who were not involved could declare their innocence and thereby avert God's judgment. A later series of curses in Deuteronomy addressed the issue of other crimes committed in secret (27:15–26).

21:10–14. Moses provided for the humane treatment of women captives taken in war. Such women must either marry an Israelite (and be provided for!), or be allowed to go free (cp. 2 Kings 5:2). Capturing prisoners of war for slaves was prohibited in ancient Israel.

21:15–17. A specific statute stipulated that a man with two wives must not show partiality to the son of his favored wife. While God allowed

Jesus alluded to the exemptions for warfare given in Deut. 20:5–8 in His parable of the great banquet. Certain persons excused themselves from attending the banquet because of pressing business or marital commitments, exemptions similar to those allowed by Moses for warfare (Luke 14:18–20; cp. Luke 18:29). Jesus preferred persons who voluntarily gave up their rights for others to those who insisted on keeping what was theirs "by right."

Understanding the spirit of the law, Jesus extended the command "you shall not kill" to "you shall not even hate or be angry" (cp. Matt. 5:21–22). Then, in the manner of Moses, he gave specific instructions about what it means not to be angry and how to make amends if you are angry (5:22–26).

Israelite men to have more than one wife, such was never His preference (cp. Gen. 2:24) and almost always resulted in tension within the home (cp. 1 Sam. 1:2–8). This statute seems to have been put in place as a result of family problems such as those faced by Jacob (cp. Gen. 29:15–30; 37:3–4).

21:18–21. The rebellion of a son against his parents was treated as a capital offense in ancient Israel because it shook the foundations of society. As state-sponsored killing, capital punishment was allowable under the terms of the sixth commandment.

21:22–23. After a man was executed for a crime, his body could be hung on a tree for public display as a deterrent to others. Moses ordered that the corpses of criminals be treated humanely and not be allowed to hang, exposed, after sundown. By implication, all dead were to be treated with respect. Joshua obeyed this law during the conquest of Canaan (Josh. 8:29; 10:26–27); the Philistines did not (1 Sam. 31:10–13).

22:1–4. Moses also addressed the unnecessary loss of property due to intentional oversight. It was a man's responsibility to restore lost property to its rightful owner if it was in his power to do so. While death through killing is not in view here, serious loss through the intention of another party is.

22:6–7. The humane treatment of persons evidenced throughout Deuteronomy applied equally to animals. In allowing the Israelites to take eggs but not a mother bird, Moses put restraints on the unnecessary loss of animal life.

The Roman practice of crucifixion was the preferred method of publicly displaying executed criminals in first-century Palestine. The Jewish law which required that those who were crucified had to be removed from the cross by sundown was based on Deut. 21:22–23 (cp. John 19:31). Paul quoted the reason for this statute, "Cursed is everyone who is hung on a tree," in showing that Jesus bore the sins of humanity on the cross (Gal. 3:13).

22:8. Finally, Moses addressed unintentional death through negligence. It was the responsibility of all Israelites to maintain their property in such a way that others would not be severely or fatally injured (cp. 2 Kings 1:2).

■ *The numerous statutes in Deuteronomy*
■ *which address the loss of life or related con-*
■ *cerns attest to the high value which God*
■ *places on human life.*

Matters Relating to the Seventh Commandment (22:9–23:18)

"You shall not commit adultery."

In its narrow focus the seventh commandment prohibits acts of sex by a person who is already married to someone else. It also has in mind all other forms of sexual purity, within the marriage bond or without, and anything that makes for good, trusting, and wholesome relationships. The key elements in this commandment are faithfulness and purity.

In Deuteronomy Moses connected the seventh commandment to holiness. The basic idea behind holiness is separation from things which fall short of God's standards of purity. God demands that all areas of life, whether in the family or the social, national, or religious spheres, be pure.

22:9–11. To introduce the seventh commandment, Moses provided specific statutes which required that things found in separate states in nature not be mixed by people. This included transvestism (22:5). Apparently Moses provided these illustrations in order to show Israel

The command not to kill presupposes the sanctity of life (cp. Gen. 1:26–27; 9:1–7; Ps. 8:5–8). Human life is precious to God and should not be harmed in any way. Any activities which are careless with human life are to be avoided. Bad driving and poor eating habits needlessly risk lives. Racial discrimination scorns people for whom Christ died. Insulting and taunting words, and bearing grudges, are not worthy of God's people.

God chose the marriage relationship as a means of expressing the intimacy which He shares with His people. No prophet better understood this than Hosea, who was commanded by God to marry an unfaithful woman (Hos. 1:2). Hosea's marriage illustrated the covenant which God had established with His people. Although Hosea had a right to divorce his wife, he did not do so but loved and forgave her (Hos. 3:1). Similarly, out of love God bypassed His right to divorce His unfaithful people (see Deut. 6:14–15; 7:6–8; Hos. 3:1).

Assembly of the Lord

The phrase *assembly of the Lord* refers not to membership in Israel but to participation in the formal gathering of God's people as a community of believers for festivals and public worship.

what it meant to live holy, separate lives. The logic of Moses in these commands is not altogether clear; perhaps he meant to preserve the order of creation in which living things were made "according to their various kind" (Gen. 1:11–12, 21, 24).

22:13–30. Moses provided several statutes detailing acts of sexual impurity outside of marriage. These include pre-marital sex (22:13–21), unchastity (22:22), seduction (22:23–24), rape (22:25–29) and incest (22:30). Similar commands had been given in Leviticus (Lev. 20:10–21). Generally speaking, if a person, male or female, entered into such sexual relations willingly, they were to be put to death. However, if a man raped an unbetrothed woman, he was to be fined and had to marry her, thus protecting her welfare.

23:1. For Moses, it was a short step from sexual purity to the types of purity which qualified an ancient Israelite to enter "the assembly of the Lord" (23:1–3, 8). Leviticus had listed several physical handicaps which disqualified Israelite men from participating in certain forms of public worship (Lev. 21:16–24). Of these, Moses mentioned only emasculation in Deuteronomy, probably because it involved the mark of circumcision which was to be a male's sign of participation in God's covenant (see Gen. 17:9–14).

23:2–8. Other criteria of disqualification had to do with a man's birth. Persons who were born illegitimately, or who were from the nations of Ammon or Moab, were also excluded from full participation in the assembly of God's people. Edomites, however, were not excluded, since they descended from Esau, the brother of Jacob, who was the ancestor of Israel (Gen. 25:21–26).

23:9–14. Moses included matters relating to personal hygiene in his elaboration of the seventh commandment because the same physical organs are involved in each case (Lev. 15:16–18; 22:4). The implication is not that the various acts of emission described by Moses are impure in and of themselves, but that there is a proper time and place for such things.

23:15–16. The humane treatment of slaves in ancient Israel included runaways, who were to be granted asylum. The assumption is that the masters of these slaves were non-Israelites who lived outside of Israel. The connection of this statute to the other laws of purity is somewhat loose. Evidently Moses included this statute here to show that for Israel, purity of life had ramifications greater than simple sexual conduct; it included social and economic relationships as well.

23:17–18. Moses' final statute relating to the seventh commandment prohibited cult prostitution by women and men. The money earned by such practices was not to be used as offerings in the temple.

■ *As God's own people, Israel was to be holy.*
■ *Among other things, this means that all*
■ *human relationships are to be kept pure.*

By every indication, cult prostitution was widespread among the ancient Near Eastern fertility religions. Canaanite religious rites included sexual activity by male and female priests in order to ensure that the land would be fertile for the upcoming year. Israel's great apostasy at Baal Peor had involved cult prostitution (Num. 25:1–5; Deut. 4:3–4).

Jesus spoke to the heart of the seventh commandment when He said that a man who looks at a woman with lust commits adultery in his heart (Matt. 5:27–30). Paul taught that because our bodies are temples of the Holy Spirit, sexual union of any kind outside of marriage is wrong (1 Cor. 6:16–20).

In ancient Babylon during the time of Nebuchadnezzar, loans were sometimes made without interest and other times made with interest rates charged as high as 23 percent.

Matters Relating to the Eighth Commandment (23:19–24:7)

"You shall not steal."

The eighth commandment focuses on matters of economic justice. Moses sought to instill in God's people a spirit of honesty, generosity and good will. He recognized that stealing involves much more than the overt act of taking someone else's property. At its heart, theft betrays trust in God to provide what is necessary for life.

23:19–20. Moses' first statute related to stealing required that loans within Israel be transacted interest-free. Interest, however, could be charged on loans made to foreigners. Because God had given freely to Israel (Lev. 25:35–38), it was considered the same as theft for an Israelite to charge his fellow citizen interest on a loan.

23:21–23. Moses included vows in his exhortation of the eighth commandment as an example of stealing from God. A vow was to be made voluntarily, but once spoken, it was to be fulfilled promptly and completely. As an extension of this statute, the writer of Proverbs called for the prompt payment of all debts (Prov. 3:27–28).

When Jesus' disciples picked grain to eat while walking through a grain field, the Pharisees criticized them for breaking the Sabbath (Matt. 12:1–7). Jesus responded that the ethical, humanitarian concern for the Law overrode a strict adherence to the letter of the Law. Jesus showed how Moses intended the Law to be used wisely, with the good of people in mind.

23:24–25. Israel was to be a caring community in the Promised Land. Those with the means to engage in agricultural pursuits had a responsibility to care for those who could not, or for hungry travellers passing through the area. Moses therefore granted the right to take sufficient produce from a field belonging to someone else to make a single meal; anything more would be stealing (Deut. 24:19–22).

24:1–5. Moses' statute on divorce prohibited a man from remarrying a woman who had been divorced twice, once by himself and later by another man. This law was quite specific and did not cover all instances of divorce. Further, it neither condemned nor condoned divorce but simply recognized that divorce existed. Jesus accepted Moses' allowance of divorce only for reasons of unfaithfulness, but taught that from the beginning God had never intended divorce to take place at all (Matt. 5:31–32; 19:7–9; cp. Gen. 2:24).

Moses may have included this statute on divorce in his discussion of the eighth commandment because divorce involves disputes about property rights, or because by wrongly remarrying a divorced woman, a man commits adultery, thereby "stealing" her from her rightful husband.

To this statute Moses appended an exemption from military service for a newlywed (see Deut. 20:7). By serving and perhaps dying in war, a man is "stolen" from his wife. Again, Moses' humanitarian concern is evident in the law.

24:6–7. Moses also prohibited kidnapping and taking an upper millstone as collateral for a loan, thereby depriving a debtor from his livelihood. In each case, the theft involved stealing life.

In the Sermon on the Mount, Jesus showed how the sixth through ninth commandments must be kept from the heart. He explained the inward dimension of "You shall not kill," then of "You shall not commit adultery," then mentioned divorce, then explained, "You shall not bear false witness" (Matt. 5:21–37). By mentioning divorce in the "You shall not steal" slot of the Ten Commandments, Jesus, like Moses, made an important connection between the two.

- Moses' concern for the worth of the individual is shown in his protection of property rights and the right to life.

Matters Relating to the Ninth Commandment (24:8–25:4)

"You shall not give false testimony against your neighbor."

The ninth commandment forbids false testimony spoken against a friend in court. In its broader application, the commandment prohibits all untruthful speech, for by lying the reputation of another person is invariably harmed or destroyed.

In connection with the ninth commandment, Moses established several statutes aimed at protecting the dignity, or reputation, of persons. Based on content, he placed these laws in an order which followed the accepted ranking of social status in ancient Israel: first a leper (24:8–9), then a debtor (24:10–13), a poor debtor (24:14–15), an indigent (24:17–22), a criminal (25:1–3) and finally an animal (25:4).

24:8–9. Miriam had slandered her brother Moses and been struck by leprosy as a result (cp. Num. 12:1–15). If an attack of leprosy should break out again, Moses warned Israel to submit to the instructions of the Levitical priests, who had the authority to treat and declare as cured (or "clean") persons who contracted the disease (Lev. 13:1–59).

24:10–13. Two statutes upheld the dignity of a debtor. A creditor was forbidden to enter a debtor's house and seize whatever item he had put up as security for the loan. If the pledged item were a cloak, the outer garment used as a bed for sleeping, it must be returned each night.

24:14–15. The dignity of a poor hired servant could be maintained by paying him each day for the work he performed. In the ancient Near East, this pay usually included his daily meal. No person should have to beg for what is their due.

24:16. Moses established the individual worth of each person by holding everyone responsible for their own sins.

24:17–22. The concern for justice due those who were on the margin of society is a common theme in Deuteronomy (see 1:17; 10:17–19; 16:18–20). Moses commanded farmers to leave some produce in the field at harvest time. By allowing the poor, the widows, and the sojourners to come in to the fields and glean, these indigent would have a means of providing for themselves without the indignity of begging.

The story of Ruth is a wonderful illustration of the socio-economic system of ancient Israel operating the way it was supposed to work. Ruth, a sojourner, was able to provide for herself and her widowed mother by gleaning in the fields of Boaz, a wealthy farmer from Bethlehem.

25:1–3. Even the criminal in ancient Israel was to have his dignity as a person maintained. If guilty of a crime which deserved the punishment of beating, a man was to receive no more than forty lashes. If more than that were administered, "your brother will be degraded in your eyes" (25:3).

25:4. At creation God placed animals under the responsible care of people (Gen. 1:28). For this reason, domesticated animals were not to be overworked or deprived of food.

The apostle Paul used Deut. 25:4 as evidence that those who preach the gospel have a right to expect their congregations to provide for their welfare (1 Cor. 9:3–9; 1 Tim. 5:17–18).

■ *Every person, regardless of their perceived*
■ *status in society, has great worth to God. For*
■ *this reason, their dignity must be protected at*
■ *all times.*

Matters Relating to the Tenth Commandment (25:5–19)

"You shall not covet."

By prohibiting covetousness, the tenth commandment goes to the heart of the other nine. To covet is to desire something that someone else has the exclusive right to hold. While the other commandments speak primarily of actions, the tenth begins with a person's thoughts and intentions. Under the umbrella of the tenth commandment, Moses provided

In some ways the marriage of Boaz to Ruth fulfills the requirements of levirate marriage as set forth in Deuteronomy. Boaz sought to marry Ruth because her husband had died, but he had first to secure that right from a male relative who was nearer Ruth's dead husband than he (Ruth 4:1–10). A clearer example of levirate marriage is found in Gen. 38:1–11.

The Sadducees used a hypothetical case of levirate responsibility to try to prove to Jesus that life after death was "unworkable" and hence didn't exist (Mark 12:18–27). Jesus replied that in heaven, persons "neither marry nor are given in marriage," thereby undercutting their argument.

statutes for situations in which intention played a primary role.

25:5–10. The custom of levirate marriage allowed a man to inherit his dead brother's property and manage it for his widow. In this way, the family property would remain intact. As part of the arrangement, the man would marry his brother's widow and any male children they would have would be counted as the sons of her dead husband. Moses institutionalized this custom in Deuteronomy and provided a means for recourse if the living brother refused to fulfill his levirate duties. It was wrong to "covet your neighbor's wife," but it was equally wrong to refuse "your brother's wife" if her welfare became your responsibility.

25:11–12. In a related case, Moses said that a woman who seized the genitals of a man in a fight (and, by implication, sought to hinder his ability to sire children) should be punished.

25:13–16. Finally, Moses spoke of the need to have just weights and measures. Moses' concern for social and economic justice, a theme prominent throughout his sermon, also provided the content of his last statute. All forms of dishonesty are, at the core, acts of the heart.

In order to illustrate the depravity of covetousness, Moses reminded Israel of their encounter with the Amalekites in the wilderness (25:17–19; cp. Exod. 17:8–16). Looking for spoil, the Amalekites ambushed Israel at a most vulnerable moment. Moses commanded that when Israel entered the Promised Land, they should destroy the Amalekites (cp. 1 Sam. 15:1–33).

■ *The tenth commandment speaks of covetous-*
■ *ness, an attitude of the heart. In doing so, it*
■ *provides an opportunity to see the internal*
■ *dimension of the other nine.*

CELEBRATING THE COVENANT (DEUT. 26:1–19)

As a conclusion to his second sermon, Moses called on Israel to remember to provide offerings for the Levites and thereby celebrate life in the Promised Land.

An Offering to God of Firstfruits and Tithes (26:1–15)

Moses had commanded Israel to bring the first (and best) produce harvested in their vineyards, orchards and fields to Jerusalem every year during the Festival of Weeks (Exod. 23:16; 34:22; Num. 28:26–31; Deut. 16:9–12). This offering was to support the Levites, who had no landed inheritance (12:6–19; 14:22–27; 18:3–5). By offering these gifts to the priests, Israel, like a vassal king, could pay homage to their sovereign Lord.

This was essentially a harvest celebration. "Weeks" was used of the period of grain harvest from the barley harvest to the wheat harvest. It was celebrated seven complete weeks, or fifty days, after Passover and so was given the name Penecost.

In a special ceremony, the offerer was to place some of his firstfruits in a basket and hand it to the priest, who would then place it before the altar in the temple (26:2–4). The one bringing the offering was to recite a creed recalling the gracious acts by which God delivered Israel from Egypt and brought them into their bounteous Promised Land (26:5–11).

Similarly, when an Israelite brought the third-year tithe of his produce to the Levites (Deut. 14:28–29) he was to offer a confession to God (26:12–15). This time, rather than rehearsing God's past acts of kindness, he was to declare his obedience to the terms of the covenant and ask God to respond by blessing His people.

■ *Moses expected Israel to bring offerings to the*
■ *priests in Jerusalem every year as evidence of*
■ *their ongoing grateful response to the terms of*
■ *God's covenant. In this way, God, His cove-*
■ *nant, His people, and the Promised Land were*
■ *inextricably bound to one another.*

A Charge to Obey God (26:16–19)

"I will make you a great nation, and I will bless you. . . And in you all families of the earth shall be blessed."

Genesis 12:2–3, NASB

Moses ended his second sermon with a charge for Israel to obey God. This charge summed up the reason for the covenant stipulations which Moses had laid out before Israel. That reason was found in the relationship which God had established between Himself and Israel and in responsibilities which each undertook to maintain their relationship.

It was Israel's responsibility to accept the Lord as God, to walk in His ways, to keep His statutes, and to obey His voice with all their heart and soul (26:16–17). God, on the other hand, promised to take Israel as His own special possession, elevate them above all other nations, and make them into a holy people (26:18–19; cp. Gen. 12:1–2; Exod. 19:5–6).

■ *In his second sermon, Moses outlined the*
■ *responsibilities of the covenant relationship*
■ *between God and Israel. As God promised, so*
■ *He would do. As Israel promised, so they*
■ *should do.*

QUESTIONS TO GUIDE YOUR STUDY

1. How did Moses teach Israel that the first four commandments, those which deal with man's relationship with God, have an ethical dimension?

2. How did Moses teach Israel that each of the commandments has an inward, heart-oriented dimension?

3. Why was it important for Israel to centralize their worship of God in one place, Jerusalem?

MOSES' THIRD SERMON   - - - - -

THE CONSEQUENCES OF OBEDIENCE (DEUT. 27:1–29:1)

In accordance with the vassal treaty format by which Moses structured the Book of Deuteronomy (see "Introduction, Structure and Content"), his third sermon outlined the consequences which Israel faced for keeping or breaking the covenant. These consequences are described as "blessings" and "curses."

The Covenant Renewal Ceremony (Deut. 27:1–26)

Once Israel had entered the land of Canaan, they were to ratify the covenant in a formal ceremony on Mount Ebal and Mount Gerazim. Moses instructed Israel to build an altar of unhewn stones (cp. Exod. 20:22–26) on Mount Ebal and erect next to it large plastered stones on which "all the words of this law," probably the Ten Commandments, were to be written (27:2–8).

The city of Shechem, located in the heart of Canaan, was nestled in a narrow valley overshadowed by Mount Ebal to the north and Mount Gerazim to the south. Shechem was a powerful Canaanite city-state that had figured prominently in the stories of the patriarchs (Gen. 12:6; 33:18; 34:1–31; 35:4; 37:12–14). Archaeologists have uncovered a structure on Mount Ebal which is thought by some to be the altar which Joshua built for the covenant renewal ceremony.

Moses then gave instructions for six tribes to stand on Mount Gerazim and six to stand on Mount Ebal. When the Levites recited the blessings which God would bestow should Israel keep the law, those on Mount Gerazim were to shout "Amen!" Upon hearing the curses which would befall Israel if they disobeyed, those on Mount Ebal were to shout "Amen!" In this way, each Israelite was to affirm his own responsibility to keep the covenant and acknowledge ahead of time the consequences of his behavior (cp. Neh. 5:13).

Before providing a general list of blessings and curses which would befall Israel in the land of Canaan, Moses cited twelve specific curses which were to be recited by the Levites to those standing on Mount Ebal, and to which Israel should respond "Amen!" (27:15–26). Each of the twelve curses covered a situation not specifically mentioned in the covenant stipulations previously given by Moses (chapters 12–25). In addition, each curse related to a sin committed in secret or without witnesses. Because such covenant infractions could not be judged by man, those who committed them were considered "cursed," that is, judged by God. By responding "Amen," each Israelite placed himself under the curse should he commit secret sins.

After the conquest of the southern portion of Canaan, Joshua led the Israelites to Mount Ebal and Mount Gerazim, where they renewed the covenant according to the instructions of Moses. (Josh. 8:30–35).

■ *By participating in a covenant renewal cere-*
■ *mony once in the Promised Land, each Isra-*
■ *elite committed himself to the terms of the*
■ *covenant and promised to obey its statutes.*

Blessings and Curses (Deut. 28:1–29:1)

The blessings and curses recorded in Deuteron-omy 28 may have been the ones spoken at the covenant renewal ceremony at Mount Ebal and Mount Gerazim (see Josh. 8:33–34). The number of verses which describe the curses outnumber those describing the blessings four to one, a sure indication that Moses needed to warn Israel about the consequences of their future disobedience (Deut. 31:16–18, 27).

Blessings for Obedience (28:1–14)

The blessings for obedience promised well-being for Israel. They were quite comprehensive, cover-ing all aspects of Israel's social, economic, and national life. God promised that Israel would be "set ... high above all the nations on earth" (28:1), an indication of their prosperity at home and abroad. Because ancient Israel was an agrar-ian society, many of these blessings centered on the abundant fertility of their land, flocks and herds (28:3–5, 8, 11–12). They are reminiscent of the general blessing to "be fruitful and increase" which God placed on mankind in the Garden of Eden (Gen. 1:28). Others focused on Israel's enhanced reputation among the nations (28:7, 10, 13), a partial fulfillment of the promise which God had made to Abraham four centuries earlier that "all peoples on earth will be blessed through you" (Gen. 12:3).

The vicinity of Shechem continued to play a prominent role in biblical history. Joshua renewed the covenant a second time when he gave his farewell address there (Josh. 24:1–28). Gideon's son Abimelech tried to establish a kingdom in Shechem (Judg. 9:1–57). Eventually Shechem became the first capital of the Northern Kingdom of Israel (1 Kings 12:25). The valley between Mount Ebal and Mount Gerazim became the homeland of the Samaritans, and it was at Sychar, near ancient Shechem, that Jesus met the woman at the well (John 4:1–42).

The Hebrew word *bless* comes from a word meaning "to bend the knee" or "kneel." A blessing, when spoken by a person, is an expression that God's favor might rest upon another. When spoken by God, a blessing is the promised bestowal of favor or goodness on elements of His creation. When a person blesses God, the literal sense of bending the knee in adoration is primary.

Under the leadership of strong, godly kings, the Southern Kingdom of Judah was peaceful and prosperous. The biblical writers described the reigns of such kings in terms consistent with the blessings which Moses listed in Deuteronomy 28 (see 1 Kings 4:29–34; 9:26–10:25; 2 Chron. 26:10).

These blessings were far from automatic, however. Moses began and ended the list of blessings with a conditional "if" (28:1, 13–14). The blessings were contingent on Israel's obedience to the covenant stipulations which Moses enumerated in his second sermon (chaps. 12–25).

■ *If Israel was faithful to God and the covenant*
■ *relationship which He established with*
■ *Israel, He would respond by blessing them in*
■ *tangible ways.*

Curses for Disobedience (28:15–29:1)

The curses for disobedience worked to reverse or undo the blessings which Moses had just stated (28:16–19; cp. 28:3–6). Like the blessings, their enactment would be a direct result of Israel's response to God's covenant stipulations (28:15, 45, 47, 58).

The curses of Deuteronomy foresee the exile of Judah to Babylon in the sixth century B.C. (see 2 Kings 25:1–26; Ps. 137; Lam. 1–5). Because Israel had been delivered from slavery in Egypt, Moses described the future Exile in terms of a return to Egypt (28:68; cp. 28:27). The emphasis on exile at the end of the Pentateuch echoes the exile which took place at the beginning of the Pentateuch. After disobeying God, Adam and Eve were exiled from the garden of Eden, their "Promised Land," to a land which had been placed under God's curse (Gen. 3:17, 22–24). However, because God was faithful to Adam and Eve after their fall, Israel could be sure that He would remain faithful whenever they, too, would fall.

- *For Israel, the result of disobedience would*
- *be catastrophic. Their land, their families,*
- *and their very beings would be affected*
- *terribly.*

QUESTIONS TO GUIDE YOUR STUDY

1. For ancient Israel, what did it mean to be blessed or cursed by God? What does it mean today?

2. Why was it important for each Israelite to say "amen!" personally to the covenant blessings and curses?

3. In light of the subsequent history of ancient Israel, how "exact" were the curses of Deuteronomy 28?

MOSES' FOURTH SERMON - - - - -

LOOKING TO THE FUTURE (DEUT. 29:2–30:20)

Moses had provided Israel with the necessary statutes to order and guide their life in the Promised Land, and had warned Israel of the consequences of their behavior once there. Moses now began to make final preparations for Israel's entrance into Canaan. His fourth sermon focused on covenant renewal (29:10–12). In it he called on Israel to make a conscious decision to follow God.

An Appeal to Covenant Faithfulness (Deut. 29:2–29)

Moses began his fourth sermon by summarizing the content of his first sermon (cp. 1:1–4:43).

"To Bless" "To Curse"

While the Hebrew language has one word for "to bless," there are six words which can be translated "to curse," each with its own nuance of meaning. The word for "curse" used in Deut. 28:15–19 means to bind or render powerless to resist. That is, once cursed by God, there was nothing Israel could do in their own strength to restore their land or their fortunes.

Moses summed up the result of the curses in verse 20: "The Lord will send on you curses, confusion and rebuke (or 'frustration') in everything you put your hand to, until you are destroyed and come to sudden ruin." He then explained in graphic detail what this "confusion and frustration" would entail.

Many of the curses which Moses called down upon Israel are actually actions which are exactly the opposite of those called for by the covenant statutes (see 28:30 and 20:5–7; 28:44 and 15:6). That is, for disobeying the terms of the covenant, Israel would have done to them what they did (but shouldn't have done!) to others. This "reversal of fortunes" became a prominent theme in the biblical prophets (see Isa. 33:1; Hab. 2:6–17) and lies behind the Golden Rule: "Do to others what you would have them do to you" (Matt. 7:12).

Toward the end of Israel's existence as a nation, many who lived in Jerusalem believed that city would never be conquered by foreign armies. God, after all, had promised to protect His city and His people (see Ps. 132:13–14). Through Jeremiah, God responded to such claims with words that echoed Deuteronomy: "If you really change your ways and your actions and deal with each other justly . . . then I will let you live in this place, in the land I gave your forefathers for ever and ever" (Jer. 7:5–7).

By His mighty acts of deliverance, God had brought Israel out of Egypt (29:2–4), led and provided for His people in the wilderness (29:5–6), defeated Sihon and Og in Transjordan (29:7), and allowed the tribes of Reuben and Gad and the half-tribe of Manasseh to settle in their land (29:8). Now Israel stood to inherit the promises which God had made to Abraham, Isaac, and Jacob (29:13; cp. Gen. 12:1–3).

Because of what God had done in the past, Israel's only proper response was to remain faithful to the covenant which he had established with them (29:9). Moses made his appeal for covenant faithfulness to all Israel—old and young, native born, sojourner and those not yet born—who stood with him on the plains of Moab (29:10–11, 14–15). His eye was clearly on the future.

Moses spoke pointedly to anyone who might suppose that they would automatically receive the benefit of God's grace simply by living within the community of God's people, thinking "I will be safe, even though I persist in going my own way" (29:19). Moses called such people a root bearing poisonous and bitter fruit (29:18). As their just reward, God would single them out for a punishment so severe that it would be remembered for generations to come (29:20–28).

In fact, Moses foresaw that, as the result of individual acts of unfaithfulness, the entire Promised Land would one day become as if sick with disease (29:22–23), and its people taken into exile (29:28). If Israel would not voluntarily teach the nations how to follow God, they would instead learn about God by witnessing His punishment of Israel.

■ *Moses called on each and every Israelite to*
■ *be faithful to God and His covenant. God's*
■ *blessings are not automatic but require indi-*
■ *vidual commitment.*

A Call to Decision (Deut. 30:1–20)

Deuteronomy 29 ends on a note of sorrow, but Deuteronomy 30 begins with a word of hope. After being uprooted from their land—a land which they hadn't even entered yet—Israel could still return to God and be forgiven (30:2–3). Moses saw a day when God would circumcise Israel's heart so they *really could* love Him with all their heart and soul, and live (30:6; cp. 6:5; 10:16). Only then would God bless His people so that they would be "most prosperous" (30:9).

The implication is clear. Moses knew that Israel, by their own strength, could never keep the covenant which God had set before them at Mount Sinai and which Moses had so carefully preserved in the Book of Deuteronomy. Yet God's people were still called to obedience and faith in Him.

If an Israelite refused to be circumcised—an unheard of choice!—he thereby refused to participate in God's covenant. If he was circumcised but did not want to hear God or obey Him, it was as if he had "uncircumcised ears" (Jer. 6:10) or an "uncircumcised heart" (Jer. 9:26). According to the biblical prophets, such a person might just as well have been uncircumcised in a physical sense. Moses looked forward to a day when God would circumcise every Israelite's heart so that, as an expression of their love

The writer of Hebrews encouraged the early church in covenant faithfulness by appealing to "so great a cloud of witnesses" who had remained faithful under adverse circumstances in times past (Heb. 11:1–12:1, KJV). In a reference to the spiritually lazy of Deut. 29:18, he cautioned, "See to it that no one misses the grace of God and that no bitter root grows up to cause trouble and defile many" (Heb. 12:15).

In Genesis 17 God provided circumcision as a sign of the covenant and a seal binding the covenant parties (God and His people) together. Being circumcised did not "save" Abraham, but only served to confirm physically his prior belief in God (see Gen. 15:6) and mark his obligation to keep God's covenant demands. This Abraham did (Gen. 26:5).

In Deut. 30:6, Moses foresaw the New Covenant spoken of in Jer. 31:31–34 and Ezek. 36:22–28: "I will put my law in their minds and write it on their hearts. I will be their God, and they will be my people" (Jer. 31:33). The apostle Paul saw that a "real Jew," someone who was truly one of God's people, was circumcised inwardly, in his heart (Rom. 2:29). People can love God only when their hearts are first changed by the cleansing work of Jesus Christ.

and faith in God, they could truly obey Him and walk in all His ways (Deut. 10:16; Jer. 4:4).

In the meantime, Moses offered Israel a clear choice: either accept good and life, or death and evil (30:15). The way was known to Israel, for in his second sermon Moses took great care to bring the commands of heaven down to the realities of life on this earth (30:11–14). In rejecting the good of Eden, Adam and Eve chose death over life (Gen. 1:31; 2:17; 3:19). Now, like that primordial couple, each Israelite must also choose to follow God or reject Him (30:16–18). God called creation itself to witness Israel's decision (30:19). If Israel should choose against God, the very land into which they were entering would turn against them.

- Everyone has to decide whether or not to fol-
- low God. Ultimately, no one can follow God
- until God first changes, or "circumcises,"
- their heart.

QUESTIONS TO GUIDE YOUR STUDY

1. How did Moses' warnings about being uprooted from the Promised Land prepare Israel for life in that land? What was Israel's response as the Babylonian Exile loomed on the horizon?

2. What does it mean to have a "circumcised heart?"

3. How does knowing that Moses wrote Genesis help us understand why he said what he said in Deuteronomy?

CONCLUDING REMARKS
(DEUT. 31:1–34:12)

The Book of Deuteronomy concludes with charges by Moses to Israel and Joshua, a poetic account of the mighty acts of God, Moses' blessing on the tribes of Israel, and a narrative account of Moses' death.

Leadership and Guidance for the Future (Deut. 31:1–29)

Although Moses would not enter the Promised Land, his legacy would live on through new leadership and the written law which he delivered to Israel.

God as Israel's True Leader (31:1–8)

Moses, now 120 years old, was about to die, and the task of taking Israel into Canaan belonged to Joshua. Moses encouraged Joshua in his task by reminding him that it was really the Lord who was leading Israel (31:3, 6, 8). God would hand the Canaanites over to Joshua just as He had delivered Sihon and Og to Moses (31:4–5; cp. 2:24–3:11). The land was truly a gift from God; Joshua had only to reach out and take it.

Moses told Israel to "be strong and courageous" (31:6), then repeated that charge to Joshua (31:7; cp. 3:21–22). After Moses died, God encouraged Joshua by speaking the same words to him three times (Josh 1:6–7, 9).

■ *With God as their true leader, Israel need*
■ *have no fear as they cross the Jordan River to*
■ *receive their Promised Land.*

God's Instructions to Be Preserved and Read (31:9–13)

The writer of Hebrews cited part of Moses' charge to Israel and Joshua, "I will not fail you or forsake you," in encouraging the early church to live contentedly, without being obsessed with financial well being (Heb. 13:5; cp. Deut. 31:6, 8).

It was important that a man of Joshua's qualifications lead Israel into Canaan, but that wasn't enough to ensure that Israel would remain faithful to God. Israel instead needed an ongoing witness to God's covenant. That, too, was provided by Moses.

Moses wrote down "this law," probably the covenant stipulations of Deuteronomy 5–25 together with the blessings and curses of chapters 27–28, and entrusted it to the priests with instructions for its future use (31:9). Every seven years, as Israel would assemble before God in Jerusalem at the Feast of Tabernacles to mark the year of release (Deut. 15:1–18), the priests were to read the Law so that the people could "listen and learn to fear the LORD your God and follow carefully all the words of this law" (31:12). In this way, every generation would commit themselves anew to participating in God's covenant (31:13).

The only recorded instance of the Law being publicly read during the Feast of Tabernacles is in Neh. 8:13–9:38. This took place after the walls of Jerusalem had been rebuilt following the Jews' return from the Babylonian Exile. After the Law was read, the people covenanted together to keep its statutes, then put it in writing and placed their seal upon it (Neh. 9:38).

■ *Moses commanded that the Law be read pub-*
■ *licly every seven years to ensure that it be*
■ *kept. Unfortunately, this was seldom done.*

Joshua as Israel's New Leader (31:14–23)

God then told Moses to bring Joshua to the tent of meeting (the tabernacle) where he was to be commissioned as the new leader of Israel (31:14–15). For the first time during the wilderness wandering experience, God spoke directly to Joshua rather than through Moses: "Be strong and of good courage!" (31:23; cp. Josh. 1:6–9). The transfer of leadership was under way.

During the commissioning service, God warned Moses that after his death, Israel would surely break the covenant (31:16–18; cp. 4:25–31; 7:1–4). To help prevent this from happening, God gave Moses a song to teach Israel. That song, recorded in Deuteronomy 32, was intended to instruct Israel in the ways of God.

How often the priests read the Law to Israel throughout their history is unknown; the evidence from the books of Kings and Chronicles suggests that it was seldom at best. During the reign of Josiah, the high priest Hilkiah found "the book of the law," which many scholars think was Deuteronomy, during temple repairs (2 Kings 22:8–20). It had evidently been lost for years. Upon hearing the Law, Josiah led a revival and instituted reforms throughout the land based on the religious and ethical instructions contained in Deuteronomy.

■ *God commissioned Joshua to replace Moses*
■ *as Israel's leader.*

God's Instructions to Be Preserved and Read (31:24–29)

Moses finally instructed the Levites to place the copy of the Law which he had written next to the ark of the covenant, the gold-covered box found in the Holy of Holies, the most sacred part of the tabernacle (temple). The written Law was thus to be a perpetual "witness" against Israel (31:24–26), bearing testimony that God's standards of holiness were not being kept.

■ *For Israel, the written Law not only provided*
■ *instruction regarding their covenant obliga-*
■ *tions, but also served to condemn them for*
■ *disobedience.*

The Song of Moses (31:30–32:47)

The Song of Moses is a brilliant composition praising the acts of God on behalf of His all-too-often erring people, Israel. As a high water mark of ancient Hebrew poetry, this song exhibits a masterful use of literary technique and artistry.

Moses was careful to portray Israel's "founding" in the wilderness as an event of creation. The words *howling waste* and *hovers* used in Deut. 32:10–11 occur also in Genesis 1:2 (there translated "without form" and "hovering"). As God made the world for people to live in and enjoy, so He made a special people to live in and enjoy His Promised Land. Appropriately, it was creation itself, "heaven and earth," that were called to witness God's gracious acts and Israel's rebellious response (32:1).

In his song, Moses recalled the period of Israel's wilderness wanderings. Rather than cite specific events from that experience, he provided an overall view, thus allowing future generations to respond, "That fits my life, too!"

The Song of Moses can be outlined as follows:

I. The Invocation of Witnesses (32:1–4)

II. The Indictment of Israel (32:5–6)

III. The Involvement of God in Israel's Past (32:7–14)

IV. The Indignation of God Against Israel (32:15–27)

V. The Invincibility of God in Spite of Israel (32:28–43)

After teaching his song to Israel, Moses exhorted the parents to instruct their children in the Law of God (32:44–46). Everything was at stake: "They are just not idle words for you—they are your life" (32:47).

■ *Moses wrote and taught Israel a song by*
■ *which the character and acts of God could be*
■ *known and remembered from generation to*
■ *generation.*

The Blessing of Moses (32:48–33:29)

In view of his impending death, Moses blessed the tribes of Israel. All in all, he saw an optimistic future for Israel. Moses elsewhere spoke of Israel's inevitable failings once they settled the Promised Land, but in this, his last will and testament, he spoke only of the good.

Moses' Impending Death (32:48–52)

As a prelude to the blessing which he would speak to the tribes of Israel, Moses was again told that he would die without entering the Promised Land (cp. 1:37; 3:23–29; 4:21; 31:2). At Meribath-kadesh God had told Moses to command water to come out of a rock so He might quench the thirst of Israel. Moses instead struck the rock with his staff as he had done on an earlier occasion (Num 20:2–13; 27:12–14; cp. Exod. 17:1–7). While a small matter in the eyes of man, Moses' disobedience had in fact "broken faith" with God, thereby compromising His holiness and proving that "all have sinned and fall short of the glory of God" (Rom. 3:23).

Moses would die and be buried on a mountain, as his brother, Aaron, had been before him (cp. Num. 20:22–29). In the awesome reverence of a desert mountaintop, each of these two great men rested near God.

- *Because of disobedience, even Moses for-*
- *feited the Promised Land. Without the grace*
- *of God, the best that people can do is still not*
- *good enough for God.*

Moses' Blessing on the Tribes of Israel (33:1–29)

Throughout the Book of Deuteronomy, Moses warned Israel about the consequences of their disobedience once they arrived in the Promised Land. His last word, however, a blessing on the tribes of Israel, was wholly optimistic. It expressed not what happened to Israel during the time of the Old Testament, but what Moses *desired* would happen—and what *could* have happened—if Israel remained faithful to God's covenant.

Jeshurun, a poetic name for Israel, is found only four places in the Bible. Of these, three are in the poems found at the end of Deuteronomy (32:15; 33:5, 26) and the other (Isa. 44:2) is in a poem about Israel's spiritual restoration. *Jeshurun* is a term of endearment that means "the Upright One." The significance of the name is not that Moses considered Israel to be upright in an absolute sense but that they kept the law and upheld justice.

Moses began and ended his blessing on Israel by offering praise to God (33:2–5, 26–29). He compared God's revelation at Mount Sinai to a brilliant desert sunrise (33:2), then declared that God's people, whom He loved, had received the law willingly (33:3). Once in their land, Israel would be safe, prosperous, and happy (33:28–29).

Jacob had blessed his sons, the ancestors of the twelve tribes of Israel, in Genesis 49. Whereas some of Jacob's blessings were more like curses (see Gen. 49:3–7), all of those spoken by Moses were favorable. Some deserve special note:

- Judah received a blessing of messianic significance by Jacob (see Gen. 49:10), but the blessing which Moses gave the tribe of Judah was no greater than those he gave to the other tribes (33:7). Rather than favor only Judah, Moses spoke well of all Israel, an indication that in the future, Judah's favored status would "infiltrate" and benefit everyone.

- The tribe of Levi, to whom God had given the priesthood (see Exod. 32:26–29; cp. Deut. 18:1–8), was given the responsibility to teach Israel the law (33:10).

- Simeon did not receive a blessing by Moses (cp. Gen. 49:5), perhaps because early on Simeon was apparently absorbed by the tribe of Judah.

- The blessing on Joseph, whose sons Ephraim and Manasseh were counted as separate tribes, reflects the bounty of their inheritance in the central hill country of Canaan (33:13–17; cp. Josh 16:1–17:18).

- Moses connected Dan with Bashan, the region of Transjordan east of the Sea of Galilee. Once in Canaan, Joshua gave Dan a small tribal inheritance along the Mediterranean Sea in an area dominated by the Philistines (Josh. 19:40–48), but Dan instead moved to a city in northern Galilee within sight of Bashan (Judg. 18:1–31).

- ■ *In spite of their certain disobedience, Moses*
- ■ *saw a great future for Israel. Some day Israel*
- ■ *would follow God completely and be blessed*
- ■ *with security, happiness, and peace.*

The Death and Legacy of Moses (34:1–12)

Finally, Moses ascended Mount Nebo, a lofty mountain above (east of) the plains of Moab (34:1). Jericho, the first city to be conquered by Joshua (cp. Josh. 6:1–27), lay due west across the Jordan River. It is not clear whether Pisgah is another name for Mount Nebo, the name of a different mountain nearby, or part of the range in which Mount Nebo is found (cp. Num. 21:20; 23:14; Deut. 3:27).

From the top of Mount Nebo God "showed [Moses] all the land" which Israel would inherit, a land which had been promised to the patriarchs over four hundred years earlier (34:2–4; cp. Gen. 12:1, 7; 13:14–15; 15:12–21; 26:3; 28:13; 35:12). The Pentateuch ended with a sure confirmation that the promises of God would be fulfilled.

Moses was buried by God in a valley somewhere in the mountains of Moab (34:6). Appropriately, his burial place was unknown; Israel belonged on the other side of the Jordan and did not need to be drawn back to a burial shrine in Moab.

Jacob's blessing in Genesis 49 was tailored to each of his sons, but had important prophetic ramifications for the tribes which descended from them. Jacob saw that the Messiah would descend from the tribe of Judah.

While the view from the traditional site of Mount Nebo today is spectacular, it is not physically possible to see every area of the Promised Land described in Deut. 34:1–3. For instance, the high central ridge of Judah hides the view of Judah "as far as the Western (i.e., Mediterranean) Sea." Whether Moses "saw" all the land physically through miraculous vision (34:7) or God simply made him aware of what was "out there" is not certain. What is clear, however, is that, unlike Israel, Moses' ability to see with "spiritual eyes" was unabated at the end of his life.

Moses received an unsurpassed epitaph (34:10–12). Although many accolades suffice, none are sufficient; perhaps all can be summed up by the phrase, "Moses, whom the LORD knew face to face" (34:10; cp. Num. 12:6–8). Moses was intimate with God, walking with him day by day. This same relationship had been known by Adam and Eve (Gen. 3:8), Enoch (Gen. 5:22–24), Noah (Gen. 6:9) and Abraham (Gen. 17:1). Moses had written the life histories of these saints, as well as his own life story. In the end, he simply desired that like them, all Israel should walk with God (cp. Deut. 5:33; 8:6; 30:16).

■ *With the death of Moses, the founding era of*
■ *ancient Israel was over. Some day another*
■ *prophet, Jesus, would arise to surpass Moses*
■ *(18:18; John 7:40), but in the meantime,*
■ *Israel had only to believe, obey, and wait.*

QUESTIONS TO GUIDE YOUR STUDY

1. In what ways do persons in the church fulfill the role of the Old Testament priests? What did the priests do that parents can do today?

2. How does the end of the Book of Deuteronomy prepare the way for the ministry of Joshua? For the conquest of Canaan? For Israel's settlement in the Promised Land?

3. Why was it important for Moses to end the Book of Deuteronomy with an optimistic view of Israel's future (chap. 33)? Was he right, or just hoping?

* * * * * * *

Deuteronomy is a book of "getting ready"—ready for a new leader, ready for a new life in a new land—ready for God. The book ends at the brink of its fulfillment, just short of its goal. The Pentateuch closes with great hope and great responsibility. Moses saw disobedience and failure, but he also saw a day when Israel could "do it right."

A modern Jewish prayer of thanksgiving expresses the spirit of the hope found in Deuteronomy:

"We thank thee, Lord our God, for having given our fathers as a heritage a pleasant, a good and spacious land; for having taken us out of the land of Egypt, for having redeemed us from the house of bondage; for Thy covenant, which Thou hast set as a seal in our flesh, for Thy Torah which Thou hast taught us, for Thy statutes which Thou hast made known to us, for the life of grace and mercy Thou hast graciously bestowed upon us, and for the nourishment with which Thou dost nourish us and feed us always, every day, in every season, and every hour."

[Grace spoken over the meal on the Sabbath, from Judah Goldin, trans., *The Grace after Meals* (New York: JTS, 1955), 9].

God is gracious in providing everything necessary for life. But He also provided the One people need most of all. Moses saw Jesus' day, and rejoiced in the prophet who surpassed even himself (18:18). Moses delivered Israel from bondage and gave them the law; Jesus delivered all people from sin and wrote the law on their hearts (Deut. 30:6). Together, we learn to follow Him.

* * * * * * *

The following is a collection of Broadman & Holman–published reference sources used for this work. They are provided here to accompany the reader's need for more specific information and/or for an expanded treatment of the Book of Deuteronomy. All of these works will greatly aid in the reader's study, teaching, and presentation of Deuteronomy. The accompanying annotations can be helpful in guiding the reader to the proper resources.

Cate, Robert L. *An Introduction to the Old Testament and Its Study*. An introductory work presenting background information, issues related to interpretation, and summaries of each book of the Old Testament.

Dockery, David S., Kenneth A. Mathews, and Robert B. Sloan. *Foundations for Biblical Interpretation: A Complete Library of Tools and Resources*. A comprehensive introduction to matters relating to the composition and interpretation of the entire Bible. This work includes a discussion of the geographical, historical, cultural, religious, and political backgrounds of the Bible.

Farris, T. V. *Mighty to Save: A Study in Old Testament Soteriology*. A wonderful evaluation of many Old Testament passages that teach about salvation. This work makes a conscious attempt to apply Old Testament teachings to the Christian life.

Holman Bible Dictionary. An exhaustive, alphabetically arranged resource of Bible-related subjects. An excellent tool of definitions and other information on the people, places, things, and events of the Book of Deuteronomy.

Holman Bible Handbook. A summary treatment of each book of the Bible that offers outlines, commentary on key themes and sections, illustrations, charts, maps, and full-color photos. This tool also provides an accent on broader theological teachings of the Bible.

Holman Book of Biblical Charts, Maps, and Reconstructions. This easy-to-use work provides numerous color charts on various matters related to Bible content and background, maps of important events, and drawings of objects, buildings, and cities mentioned in the Bible.

Honeycutt, Roy Lee, Jr. *Leviticus, Numbers, Deuteronomy* (Layman's Bible Book Commentary, vol. 3). A popular-level treatment of the book of Deuteronomy. This easy-to-use volume provides a relevant and practical perspective for the reader.

Merrill, Eugene H. *Deuteronomy* (The New American Commentary, vol. 4). A scholarly treatment that emphasizes the text of Deuteronomy, its backgrounds, theological considerations, issues in interpretation, and summaries of scholarly debates on important points.

Sandy, D. Brent, and Ronald L. Giese, Jr. *Cracking Old Testament Codes*. A guide to interpreting the literary genres of the Old Testament. This book is designed to make scholarly discussions available to preachers and teachers.

Smith, Ralph L. *Old Testament Theology: Its History, Method and Message*. A comprehensive treatment of various issues relating to Old Testament theology. Written for university and seminary students, ministers, and advanced lay teachers.